The *Revised* Index of ELT M

Introduction

Much of an EFL teacher's work consists of lesson preparation, and a large proportion of the time spent on this consists of looking for suitable materials for use in lessons. As the number of ELT publications increases considerably each year, so too does the time needed to locate suitable pieces of material. This Index provides teachers with a quick, easy-to-use reference system which will significantly reduce the amount of time and energy which they need to devote to that aspect of lesson preparation.

Clearly *The Index* is not a comprehensive guide to ELT publications; if it were, it would be too unwieldy to serve its purpose. Instead, it provides references to a wide variety of material contained in over 100 of the most useful and easily available books published since 1978. It is organised in such a way that teachers can quickly locate in those books the sections which contain the most useful and relevant pieces of material for their particular lesson preparation needs.

I would like to thank Jeff Mohamed, for his valuable editorial advice and assistance (and for having contributed the section: How To Use This Index) in the original version of the *Index of EFL Materials,* and Matthew Barnard, for the editing and presentation of the revised version.

Richard Acklam

Contents

How To Use This Index

Choosing the appropriate section

The Index is divided into five sections:

1. Grammar
2. Functions
3. Topics
4. Writing
5. Miscellaneous

Consult **Section 1. Grammar** for materials through which to introduce/practise/revise grammatical structures (eg. verb tenses, prepositions, modals). This section is divided into the categories most commonly found in popular student grammar books and the items are listed in a similar order.

Consult **Section 2. Functions** for materials through which to introduce/practise/revise functions (eg. giving advice) and functional exponents (eg. If I were you...).

Consult **Section 3. Topics** for materials through which to introduce/practise/revise vocabulary items around a topic or theme (eg. education, sport).

Consult **Section 4. Writing** for materials through which to introduce/practise/revise types and aspects of writing (eg. letters, messages, punctuation).

Consult **Section 5. Miscellaneous** contains references to useful material in other areas (eg. deducing from context; formal v. informal language; learner training).

Choosing specific areas of interest

Each section begins with a list of Contents for that section. These lists give a series of sub-headings to help you define more closely the language areas or topics which you want to introduce, practise or revise with your students.
Choose the most appropriate sub-heading and turn to the page indicated in the list of Contents. There you will find one or more entries, each referring to a part or parts of an ELT book.

> **As new books are published, you will want to update the Index. So we have left pages 93-96 blank for Reader's Notes.**

Choosing the most appropriate entries

In general the sub-headings given are sufficiently specific to allow you to select the appropriate entries without difficulty. However, some of the sub-headings are quite broad (eg. Animals). In these cases, many references will indicate which specific aspect of the topic is involved. So, under the sub-heading *Animals*, references will often carry indicators such as *Whales*, *Zoos* etc. Where no specific aspect is indicated, the entry refers to material covering either the general sub-heading topic or several aspects of it.

Knowing the type of material referred to

Entries in the Index do not specifically indicate what type of material is being referred to, ie. whether it is a reading text, a role play, a written exercise etc. However, it is usually possible to predict with accuracy the type of material concerned even if you do not have firsthand knowledge of the relevant book. The notes below will help you to make accurate predictions.

1. The title of a book frequently gives a clue to the type of material it contains. So a reference to a part of *Play Games With English* will be to a game, quiz or puzzle; a reference to *Task Listening* will be to a listening text eg. conversation, extract from TV programme etc.; a reference to *Keep Talking* will be to a discussion, role play etc.

2. The Source Publications list at the front of the Index indicates the type of material contained in the books which appear in the Index.

3. Coursebooks usually contain a wide variety of types of material.

NB:

Where a reference is to a single page, it is frequently to a single activity. Where the reference is to several pages or a unit, a number of activities are likely to be involved.

Where the reference is to a unit in a coursebook, it usually involves a whole set of activities and materials around a language area or topic (eg. a reading and/or listening text with accompanying tasks, followed by several oral/written exercises or tasks).

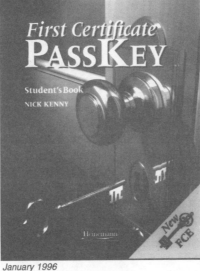

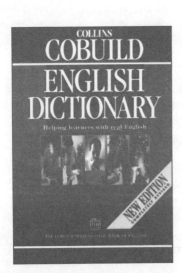

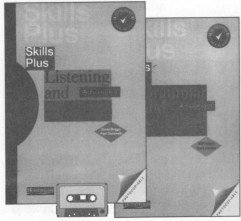

Source Publications

Coursebooks

BOOK TITLE Author(s)	PUBLISHER Date	LEVEL Comments
BLUEPRINT B.Abbs, I.Freebairn	Longman 1990-1995	4 level coursebook series (1, 2, Int, U.Int) Upper Secondary/Adult
(NEW) CAMBRIDGE ENGLISH COURSE M.Swan, C.Walter (with D.O'Sullivan)	CUP 1990-1993	4 level coursebook series (1-4)
(THE) CHOICE S.Mohamed, R.Acklam	Longman 1992-5	3 level coursebook series (Begs., Pre-Int., Int.)
DISTINCTION M.Foley, D.Hall	Longman 1993	Advanced coursebook
FIRST CERTIFICATE GOLD R.Acklam (with S.Burgess)	Longman 1996	New for the revised First Certificate exam
(NEW) FIRST CERTIFICATE MASTERCLASS S.Haines, B.Stewart	OUP 1996	Revised edition for the revised First Certificate exam
FOCUS S. O'Connell	Longman 1984,1992	3 levels (First Certificate, CAE, Proficiency)
HEADSTART B.Beaven, T.Falla (with J. and L.Soars)	OUP 1995	Absolute beginner coursebook
HEADWAY J. and L. Soars	OUP 1986-96	5 level coursebook series (Elem - Adv.)
LANGUAGE IN USE A.Doff, C.Jones	CUP 1991,1994	2 levels (Pre-Int., Int.)
LANGUAGE ISSUES G.Porter-Ladousse	Longman 1993	Advanced coursebook

LOOK AHEAD A.Hopkins, J.Potter and J.Naunton (with D.Hall and M.Du Vivier)	Longman 1994,1995	4 level coursebook series (1, 2, Int., Upper Int.)
MATTERS J.Bell, R.Gower (with G.Cunningham)	Longman 1991-6	4 level coursebook series (Elem., Pre-Int., Int., U.Int.)
MEANINGS INTO WORDS A.Doff, C.Jones, K. Mitchell	CUP 1983/84	2 levels (Int., U.Int.)
NELSON PROFICIENCY COURSE S.Morris, A.Stanton	Longman 1990	Exam coursebook
PROGRESS TO PROFICIENCY (NEW EDITION) L.Jones	CUP 1993	Exam coursebook
PROFICIENCY MASTERCLASS K.Gude, M.Duckworth	OUP 1994	Exam coursebook
REWARD S.Greenall	Heinemann 1994	3 level coursebook series (Pre-Int., Int., U.Int)
STREAMLINE (DEPARTURES/CONNECTI ONS) B.Hartley, P.Viney	OUP 1978/79	Structurally organised coursebook series (Begs. +)
THINK AHEAD TO FIRST CERTIFICATE J.Naunton	Longman 1993	Mid-Int. coursebook
THINK FIRST CERTIFICATE (REVISED) J.Naunton	Longman 1996	Revised edition for the revised First Certificate exam
TRUE TO LIFE R.Gairns, S.Redman, J.Collie, S.Slater	CUP 1995,1996	3 level coursebook series (Elem., Pre-Int., Int.)
WORKOUT P.Radley, C.Millerchip, K.Burke	Longman 1993-95	4 level coursebook series (Pre-Int. - Adv.)

The Index: *Source publications*

Supplementary Books

BOOK TITLE Author(s)	PUBLISHER Date	LEVEL Comments
(THE) ANTI-GRAMMAR GRAMMAR BOOK N.Hall, J.Shepheard	Longman 1991	Variety of practice activites focussing on tensese (Int.-Adv.)
COMMUNICATION GAMES J.Hadfield	Longman 1984,1987,1990	Games practising a variety of language areas (Elem., Int., Adv.)
CONVERSATION PIECES S.Mumford	Pergamon 1983	Semi-authentic, structurally organised listening texts (Elem.)
DISCUSSIONS THAT WORK P.Ur	CUP 1981	Range of speaking activities (all levels)
ENGLISH GRAMMAR IN USE (2nd edition) R.Murphy	CUP 1994	Students' reference grammar with exercises (Int.)
ENGLISH GRAMMAR LESSONS M.Dean	OUP 1993	Wide range of practice activities for main grammar areas with summary of key rules (U.Int.)
ENGLISH VOCABULARY IN USE M.McCarthy, F.O'Dell	CUP 1994	Students' reference and practice book (U.Int./Adv.)
ESSENTIAL GRAMMAR IN USE R.Murphy	CUP 1990	Students' reference grammar with exercises (Elem.)
EVERYDAY LISTENING AND SPEAKING (MAKING HEADWAY) S.Cunningham, P.Moor	OUP 1992,1993	Pre-Int./ Int. activities focusing on everyday spoken English

GRAMMAR GAMES (+ MORE GRAMMAR GAMES) M.Rinvolucri, P.Davis	CUP 1984,1995	Cognitive, affective and drama activities to practise a variety of grammatical areas (all levels)
GRAMMAR PRACTICE ACTIVITIES P.Ur	CUP 1988	Variety of grammar practice activities (all levels)
HELP WITH PHRASAL VERBS R.Acklam	Heinemann 1992	Topic-based approach with range of practice activities (Mid.-Int.)
KEEP TALKING F.Klippel	CUP 1984	Wide range of communicative speaking activities (Elem.-Adv.)
(THE) LISTENING FILE J.Harmer, S.Elsworth	Longman 1989	Authentic interviews (U.Int. - Adv.)
OXFORD SUPPLEMENTARY SKILLS SERIES Series ed. A.Maley	OUP 1987,1988,1992	4 x 4 skills series covering listening, speaking, reading, writing from Elem. to Adv.
PHRASAL VERBS AND IDIOMS (MAKING HEADWAY) G.Workman	OUP 1993,1995	Topic based approach with range of practice activities (U.Int./Adv.)
PLAY GAMES WITH ENGLISH 1,2,3 (Teacher's Resource Books) C.Granger	Heinemann 1993,1995	Various games and activities (Begs., Elem., Int.)
(THE) Q BOOK J.Morgan, M.Rinvolucri	Longman 1988	Activities focussing on the use of questions (Elem. - Adv.)
SPEAKING PERSONALLY G.Porter-Ladousse	CUP 1983	Quizzes and questionnaires for fluency practice (U.Int./Adv.)
START TESTING YOUR VOCABULARY P.Watcyn-Jones	Penguin 1982	A variety of vocabulary exercised (Elem.)

SURVIVAL LESSONS D.Hall, M.Foley	Longman 1990	Double-page lessons focussing on commonly problematic structures (Int. - U.Int.)
TASK LISTENING (+ ELEMENTARY TASK LISTENING) L.Blundell, J.Stokes	CUP 1981,1984	Semi-authentic listening texts (Elem., Int.)
TEST YOUR VOCABULARY (1-5) P.Watcyn-Jones	Penguin 1980-91	Variety of vocabulary exercises (Begs. - Adv.)
(ELEMENTARY/INTERME DIATE) VOCABULARY B.J.Thomas	Longman 1986,1990	Vocabulary practice organised by topic area (Elem., Int.)
(ADVANCED) VOCABULARY AND IDIOM B.J.Thomas	Longman 1989	Vocabulary practice organised by topic area (Adv.)
VOCABULARY BUILDER (1+2) B.Seal	Longman 1987, 1988	Double-page units introducing and practising different topic areas (Early/Mid.Int.)
(A) WAY WITH WORDS (1-3) S.Redman and R.Ellis	CUP 1989,1990	Various vocabulary development activities (Pre-Int. - U.Int.)
WORDBUILDER G.Wellman	Heinemann 1989	Vocabulary reference and practice book (U.Int./Adv.)
WRITING GAMES C. + J.Hadfield	Longman 1990	Various writing games and activities (Pre-Int. - Adv.)

Section 1: Grammar

This section is divided into the categories most commonly found in popular student grammar books and the items are listed in a similar order.

IMPERATIVES

Beginner/Elementary
- Blueprint One pp.117-118
- Play Games With English 1 pp.78-79
- Play Games With English 2 pp.20-21
- Streamline Departures Unit 12
- The Beginners' Choice p.57
- The New Cambridge English Course 1 p.110

Early/Mid-Intermediate
- Play Games With English 3 pp.6-7

Various
- Grammar Practice Activities pp.127-135
- More Grammar Games pp.69-70

PRESENT SIMPLE (ROUTINE) + ADVERBS OF FREQUENCY

Beginner/Elementary
- Blueprint One pp.23-24,37-38
- Conversation Pieces pp.1-28
- Elementary Communication Games No.24
- Essential Grammar In Use pp.10-15
- Headstart pp.38-42,44-47,62-65
- Headway Elementary pp.19-21
- Look Ahead 1 pp.60-61
- Play Games With English 1 pp.18-19,22-23
- Streamline Departures Units 32-37
- The Beginners' Choice p.26
- The New Cambridge English Course 1 pp.30-31,93
- True To Life Elementary pp.28,31-35

Pre-Intermediate
- Blueprint Two pp.9-10
- Headway Pre-Intermediate pp.13-15
- Language In Use Pre-Intermediate pp.16-18
- Pre-Intermediate Matters p.15
- Reward Pre-Intermediate pp.2-5
- The New Cambridge English Course 2 pp.12-15
- The Pre-Intermediate Choice pp.34-35
- Workout Pre-Intermediate pp.10-11

Early/Mid-Intermediate
- English Grammar In Use pp.4-5
- Headway Intermediate pp.1-6 [routine + states]
- Intermediate Communication Games Nos.1,5,6
- Intermediate Matters pp.11-13
- Language In Use Intermediate pp.8-9
- Meanings Into Words Intermediate pp.18-19
- New Headway Intermediate pp.15-16

Upper Intermediate
- Headway Upper Intermediate p.89
- Think First Certificate [Revised] p.13 [adverbs of frequency]
- Upper Intermediate Matters pp.10-11

Various
- Grammar Games pp.100-101,109
- Grammar Practice Activities pp.50-52,254-262

PRESENT SIMPLE v. PRESENT CONTINUOUS

Beginner/Elementary
- Essential Grammar In Use pp.16-17
- Blueprint One pp.91-92
- The New Cambridge English Course 1 p.79
- True To Life Elementary p.70

Pre-Intermediate
- Language In Use Pre-Intermediate p.25
- Look Ahead 2 p.9
- Pre-Intermediate Matters pp.14-15
- Reward Pre-Intermediate pp.10-11
- The Pre-Intermediate Choice p.35
- True To Life Pre-Intermediate pp.9-10

PRESENT SIMPLE v. PRESENT CONTINUOUS

Early/Mid-Intermediate
- English Grammar In Use pp.6-9
- Intermediate Matters p.14
- Language In Use Intermediate p.10
- New Blueprint Intermediate pp.16-17
- New Headway Intermediate pp.17-20
- Survival Lessons pp.5,36-37
- The Intermediate Choice pp.42,44
- The New Cambridge English Course 3 p.116
- Workout Intermediate p.14

Upper Intermediate
- Blueprint Upper Intermediate p.19
- English Grammar Lessons pp.8-11
- Look Ahead Upper Intermediate pp.8-9
- Upper Intermediate Matters pp.10-11

Various
- Grammar Practice Activities p.253
- The Anti-Grammar Grammar Book pp.12-13,83,20-21,92,23,97-98,24-25,99

PRESENT CONTINUOUS (NOW / 'AROUND NOW')

Beginner/Elementary
- Blueprint One pp.43-44
- Elementary Communication Games Nos.36-37
- Essential Grammar In Use pp.6-9
- Headway Elementary pp.77-79
- Look Ahead 1 pp.68-69
- Play Games With English 1 pp.12-13,16-17,38-39,54-55
- Play Games With English 2 pp.6-7
- Streamline Departures Units 21-22,25
- The Beginners' Choice p.81
- The New Cambridge English Course 1 pp.45,72-73
- True To Life Elementary pp.69-70

Pre-Intermediate
- Language In Use Pre-Intermediate pp.24-26
- Pre-Intermediate Matters p.15
- The New Cambridge English Course 2 pp.16-17
- The Pre-Intermediate Choice p.36
- True To Life Pre-Intermediate pp.9-10
- Workout Pre-Intermediate pp.18-19

Early/Mid-Intermediate
- English Grammar In Use pp.2-3
- Headway Intermediate pp.2-3
- Meanings Into Words Intermediate pp.37-42
- Play Games With English 3 pp.20-21

Various
- Grammar Practice Activities pp.246-252

PRESENT CONTINUOUS (FUTURE ARRANGEMENTS)

Beginner/Elementary
- Blueprint One pp.83-84
- Elementary Communication Games Nos.39-40
- Essential Grammar In Use pp.42-43
- Look Ahead 1 p.109
- The New Cambridge English Course 1 pp.74-75
- True To Life Elementary pp.75-77

Pre-Intermediate
- Language In Use Pre-Intermediate p.51
- Pre-Intermediate Matters pp.32-33
- The New Cambridge English Course 2 pp.72-73
- The Pre-Intermediate Choice p.81

Early/Mid-Intermediate
- English Grammar In Use pp.38-39
- Headway Intermediate pp.65-66
- Intermediate Matters p.72

PRESENT CONTINUOUS (FUTURE ARRANGEMENTS)

Intermediate
- Meanings Into Words Intermediate pp.12-13
- New Headway Intermediate pp.47-49
- Workout Intermediate p.62

PRESENT CONTINOUS (CHANGING SITUATIONS)

Beginner/Elementary
- True To Life Elementary pp.70-73

Pre-Intermediate
- The New Cambridge English Course 2 pp.18-19

Early/Mid-Intermediate
- Meanings Into Words Intermediate pp.37-39

Upper Intermediate
- First Certificate Gold p.17

Various
- The Anti-Grammar Grammar Book pp.22-23,95

PRESENT CONTINUOUS (ANNOYING HABITS)

Upper Intermediate
- Headway Upper Intermediate pp.89-90
- Look Ahead Upper Intermediate p.123
- Upper Intermediate Matters p.11

OVERVIEW OF PRESENT TENSES

Early/Mid-Intermediate
- True To Life Intermediate pp.9-11 [Present Continuous]
- Workout Intermediate pp.10,14,15

Upper Intermediate
- First Certificate Gold pp.17-18

OVERVIEW OF PRESENT TENSES contd.

Advanced
- The Nelson Proficiency Course pp.29-30
- Workout Advanced pp.10-11

Various
- The Anti-Grammar Grammar Book pp.13-15,84-86 [Present Simple],19-21,91-92 [Present Continuous]

GOING TO (FUTURE PLANS)

Beginner/Elementary
- Blueprint One pp.71-72
- Conversation Pieces pp.41-48
- Essential Grammar In Use pp.44-45
- Headway Elementary pp.83-85
- Play Games With English 1 pp.62-63,70-71
- Streamline Departures Units 27-28
- The Beginners' Choice p.51
- The New Cambridge English Course 1 pp.104-105
- True To Life Elementary pp.78-79

Pre-Intermediate
- Language In Use Pre-Intermediate pp.50-52
- Look Ahead 2 p.17
- True To Life Pre-Intermediate pp.52-53
- Pre-Intermediate Matters pp.32-33

Early/Mid-Intermediate
- English Grammar In Use pp.40-41
- Intermediate Communication Games No.13
- Intermediate Matters pp.35-36
- Meanings Into Words Intermediate p.11
- Workout Intermediate p.47

Various
- Grammar Practice Activities pp.94-105,113-116

GOING TO (PREDICTIONS / PRESENT EVIDENCE)

Beginner/Elementary
- Essential Grammar In Use pp.44-45
- Play Games With English 2 pp.28-29
- The New Cambridge English Course 1 p.106

Pre-Intermediate
- Language In Use Pre-Intermediate p.96

Early/Mid-Intermediate
- English Grammar In Use pp.40-41
- Intermediate Matters pp.35-36
- Meanings Into Words Intermediate pp.138-139
- Workout Intermediate p.47

Various
- Grammar Practice Activities pp.94-105,113-116

WILL (PREDICTIONS)

Beginner/Elementary
- Essential Grammar In Use pp.46-49
- Play Games With English 2 pp.60-61
- The Beginners' Choice pp.115-116
- The New Cambridge English Course 1 pp.112-115
- True To Life Elementary pp.150-152

Pre-Intermediate
- Blueprint Two pp.35-36
- Language In Use Pre-Intermediate pp.94-95
- Look Ahead 2 pp.108-109
- Reward Pre-Intermediate pp.28-29
- Streamline Connections Units 6,48
- True To Life Pre-Intermediate pp.104-105,130

Early/Mid-Intermediate
- Headway Intermediate p.25
- Intermediate Communication Games No. 34
- Intermediate Matters pp.35-36
- Language In Use Intermediate p.50
- Look Ahead Intermediate p.89
- Meanings Into Words Intermediate pp.136-137,140
- The Intermediate Choice p.49
- True To Life Intermediate pp.7-8

Upper Intermediate
- Meanings Into Words Upper Intermediate p.138

Various
- Keep Talking Activity No.65

WILL (PROMISES)

Pre-Intermediate
- Blueprint Two pp.35-36

Early/Mid-Intermediate
- Intermediate Communication Games No.21

WILL (FUTURE FACTS)

Beginner/Elementary
- Essential Grammar In Use pp.46-49
- True To Life Elementary p.148

Pre-Intermediate
- Headway Pre-Intermediate pp.65-67
- Streamline Connections Units 5,7,55

WILL (SPONTANEOUS DECISIONS)

Early/Mid-Intermediate
- Meanings Into Words Intermediate p.10

WILL (VARIOUS)

Beginner/Elementary
- Streamline Departures Unit 72

Pre-Intermediate
- Pre-Intermediate Matters p.56 [opinions]

Early/Mid-Intermediate
- English Grammar In Use pp.42-45
- Workout Intermediate p.51

WILL v. GOING TO

Pre-Intermediate
- Headway Pre-Intermediate pp.35-36
- Pre-Intermediate Matters pp.32-33
- Reward Pre-Intermediate pp.30-31
- The Pre-Intermediate Choice p.19
- Workout Pre-Intermediate pp.86-87 [predictions]

Early/Mid-Intermediate
- English Grammar In Use pp.46-47
- Headway Intermediate pp.24-25
- Intermediate Matters pp.35-36
- Meanings Into Words Intermediate p.9
- New Blueprint Intermediate pp.38-39
- New Headway Intermediate pp.45-47
- Play Games With English 3 pp.26-27
- The Intermediate Choice p.20
- Think Ahead to First Certificate p.87
- Workout Intermediate p.51

Upper Intermediate
- Look Ahead Upper Intermediate p.66
- Workout Upper Intermediate p.25

SHALL v. WILL

Beginner/Elementary
- Streamline Departures Unit 72
- Essential Grammar In Use pp.46-49

Early/Mid-Intermediate
- English Grammar In Use pp.42-45

Various
- The Anti-Grammar Grammar Book pp.64,138

FUTURE CONTINUOUS AND/OR FUTURE PERFECT

Early/Mid-Intermediate
- English Grammar In Use pp.48-49
- Language In Use Intermediate pp.50-51
- Meanings Into Words Intermediate p.139
- Play Games With English 3 pp.32-33 [Future Continuous]
- Think Ahead to First Certificate p.115 [Future Simple/Future Perfect]

Upper Intermediate
- Blueprint Upper Intermediate pp.81,85
- English Grammar Lessons pp.100-103
- First Certificate Gold p.93
- Look Ahead Upper Intermediate pp.98-99 [Future Continuous],112-113 [Future Perfect]
- New First Certificate Masterclass p.30
- The New Cambridge English Course 4 pp.54-55
- Think First Certificate [Revised] p.177
- Upper Intermediate Matters pp.57-58
- Workout Upper Intermediate p.95

Advanced
- Language Issues pp.19-21,63-64 [Future Continuous]

Various
- Grammar Practice Activities pp.120-121 [Future Perfect]
- The Anti-Grammar Grammar Book pp.69-73,147-150 [Future Continuous], 74-82,151-160 [Future Perfect]

OVERVIEW OF FUTURE FORMS

PAST SIMPLE

IRREGULAR VERBS

PAST CONTINUOUS

PAST CONTINUOUS contd.

- Streamline Connections Units 23,54 [setting the scene]
- The New Cambridge English Course 2 pp.28-29
- The Pre-Intermediate Choice p.73
- True To Life Pre-Intermediate pp.78-79
- Workout Pre-Intermediate pp.34-35

Early/Mid-Intermediate
- English Grammar In Use pp.12-13
- Headway Intermediate pp.14-16
- Intermediate Matters pp.19-25
- Language In Use Intermediate pp.16-17
- Look Ahead Intermediate pp.32-33
- Meanings Into Words Intermediate pp.83-88,158-160,162-163
- New Blueprint Intermediate pp.22-23
- New Headway Intermediate pp.24-26
- Survival Lessons pp.6,38-39
- The Intermediate Choice pp.36-37,39 [overview]
- The New Cambridge English Course 3 p.117
- Workout Intermediate pp.22-23

Upper Intermediate
- English Grammar Lessons pp.20-23

Advanced
- Focus On Advanced English pp.49-50

Various
- Grammar Practice Activities pp.208-212
- The Anti-Grammar Grammar Book pp.45-49,120-125

PRESENT PERFECT v. PAST SIMPLE

Beginner/Elementary
- Essential Grammar In Use pp.38-39
- Headway Elementary pp.99-102
- The New Cambridge English Course 1 p.99

Pre-Intermediate
- Headway Pre-Intermediate pp.48-51
- Look Ahead 2 p.96
- Pre-Intermediate Matters pp.44-45
- The Pre-Intermediate Choice pp.40-41
- True To Life Pre-Intermediate pp.40-41
- Workout Pre-Intermediate pp.52-53

Early/Mid-Intermediate
- English Grammar In Use pp.26-29
- Language In Use Intermediate pp.68-69
- Meanings Into Words Intermediate p.85
- Survival Lessons pp.7,40-41
- The Intermediate Choice pp.6-7
- The New Cambridge English Course 3 p.118
- Think Ahead to First Certificate p.49
- True To Life Intermediate pp.28-30
- Workout Intermediate p.39

Upper Intermediate
- Blueprint Upper Intermediate p.10
- English Grammar Lessons pp.32-35,132-135
- Headway Upper Intermediate pp.16-19
- Look Ahead Upper Intermediate pp.10-11
- Meanings Into Words Upper Intermediate p.1-3
- The New Cambridge English Course 4 p.60
- Think First Certificate [Revised] pp.30-31
- Upper Intermediate Matters p.20
- Workout Upper Intermediate pp.58-59

Advanced
- Proficiency Masterclass p.134
- The Nelson Proficiency Course p.128

Various
- The Anti-Grammar Grammar Book pp.29-33,103-107

PRESENT PERFECT (EXPERIENCE; ever/never etc.)

Beginner/Elementary
- Blueprint One pp.103-104
- Conversation Pieces pp.49-52
- Essential Grammar In Use pp.32-33
- Headway Elementary pp.99-102
- Streamline Departures Unit 65-67
- The Beginners' Choice pp.104-106
- The New Cambridge English Course 1 p.94
- True To Life Elementary pp.89,94-95

Pre-Intermediate
- Headway Pre-Intermediate pp.48-50
- Language In Use Pre-Intermediate p.70
- Look Ahead 2 pp.88-89
- Pre-Intermediate Matters pp.44-45
- Reward Pre-Intermediate pp.50-51
- The New Cambridge English Course 2 pp.44-45
- The Pre-Intermediate Choice p.40
- True To Life Pre-Intermediate p.26

PRESENT PERFECT (EXPERIENCE; ever/never etc.) contd.

Early/Mid-Intermediate
- English Grammar In Use pp.16-17
- Intermediate Matters p.28
- Workout Intermediate pp.26-7

Upper Intermediate
- Meanings Into Words Upper Intermediate pp.2-3, 6
- Upper Intermediate Matters p.20

Various
- Grammar Games pp.104-105
- Grammar Practice Activities pp.237-239

PRESENT PERFECT (RECENT PAST)

Beginner/Elementary
- Blueprint One pp.101-102
- Headway Elementary pp.100-101
- Play Games With English 2 pp.32-33
- True To Life Elementary pp.102-103

Pre-Intermediate
- Blueprint Two pp.41-42
- Language In Use Pre-Intermediate pp.68-69
- Look Ahead 2 pp.82-83
- Pre-Intermediate Matters pp.44-45
- Reward Pre-Intermediate pp.52-53
- The New Cambridge English Course 2 pp.50-51
- The Pre-Intermediate Choice pp.41-42

Early/Mid-Intermediate
- English Grammar In Use pp.14-15
- Language In Use Intermediate pp.35-36 [changes]
- Meanings Into Words Intermediate pp.51-52

PRESENT PERFECT (EVIDENT NOW/PRESENT RESULT)

Beginner/Elementary
- Essential Grammar In Use pp.30-31
- Play Games With English 2 pp.42-43

Pre-Intermediate
- Headway Pre-Intermediate pp.101-103

Early/Mid-Intermediate
- English Grammar In Use pp.26-27
- Play Games With English 3 pp.16-17

Upper Intermediate
- Upper Intermediate Matters p.21

PRESENT PERFECT (INDEFINITE PAST)

Beginner/Elementary
- Streamline Departures Unit 62

Pre-Intermediate
- Workout Pre-Intermediate pp.44-45

Early/Mid-Intermediate
- Think Ahead to First Certificate p.49

Upper Intermediate
- Upper Intermediate Matters p.20

Various
- Grammar Games pp.81-82
- The Anti-Grammar Grammar Book pp.33,108

PRESENT PERFECT (UNFINISHED PAST)

Beginner/Elementary
- Essential Grammar In Use pp.34-35
- The New Cambridge English Course 1 p.95
- Streamline Departures Unit 75

Pre-Intermediate
- Headway Pre-Intermediate pp.50-51
- Look Ahead 2 pp.90-91
- The Pre-Intermediate Choice pp.67-69
- Reward Pre-Intermediate pp.54-55
- True To Life Pre-Intermediate pp.89-91

Early/Mid-Intermediate
- English Grammar In Use pp.22-23
- Intermediate Matters p.92
- Language In Use Intermediate pp.86-88
- Think Ahead to First Certificate p.49

Various
- Grammar Games pp.28-31

PRESENT PERFECT SIMPLE (OVERVIEW)

FOR/SINCE/AGO

PRESENT PERFECT CONTINUOUS (v. SIMPLE)

PAST PERFECT SIMPLE

PAST PERFECT SIMPLE contd.

Early/Mid-Intermediate
- English Grammar In Use pp.30-31
- Intermediate Matters pp.124-126
- Language In Use Intermediate pp.76-78
- Look Ahead Intermediate pp.104-105
- Meanings Into Words Intermediate pp.160-161
- New Blueprint Intermediate p.111
- New Headway Intermediate pp.26-27
- Play Games With English 3 pp.14-15
- Survival Lessons pp.9,44-45
- The Intermediate Choice p.68
- The New Cambridge English Course 3 p.121

Upper Intermediate
- English Grammar Lessons pp.56-59
- Meanings Into Words Upper Intermediate pp.21-27
- The New Cambridge English Course 4 pp.82-83

Advanced
- Focus On Advanced English pp.141-142
- Language Issues pp.39-40

Various
- Grammar Games pp.106-107
- Grammar Practice Activities pp.206-207
- More Grammar Games pp.58-59,146,168-172
- The Anti-Grammar Grammar Book pp.50-57,126-131

PAST PERFECT CONTINUOUS

Early/Mid-Intermediate
- English Grammar In Use pp.32-33
- Intermediate Matters pp.125-126
- Play Games With English 3 pp.50-51

Upper Intermediate
- Blueprint Upper Intermediate p.39
- English Grammar Lessons pp.56-59
- Meanings Into Words Upper Intermediate p.23
- Upper Intermediate Matters p.29 (Past Perfect Simple v. Continuous]

Various
- The Anti-Grammar Grammar Book pp.58-61,133-135

NARRATIVE TENSES

Early/Mid-Intermediate
- Intermediate Communication Games No.9
- Language In Use Intermediate pp.76-78
- New Headway Intermediate pp.24-28
- Play Games With English 3 pp.24-25
- Think Ahead to First Certificate pp.20,32

Upper Intermediate
- Blueprint Upper Intermediate pp.38-39
- First Certificate Gold pp.41-43
- Headway Upper Intermediate pp.45-46
- Look Ahead Upper Intermediate pp.42-43,55
- The New Cambridge English Course 4 pp.96-97
- Think First Certificate [Revised] pp.46-47
- Upper Intermediate Matters p.28
- Workout Upper Intermediate p.31

Advanced
- Distinction p.18
- Headway Advanced p.31

Various
- The Anti-Grammar Grammar Book pp.62-63,137

TIME EXPRESSIONS

Beginner/Elementary
- Headway Elementary pp.56-57
- Start Testing Your Vocabulary p.31

Pre-Intermediate
- Headway Pre-Intermediate pp.66-67
- Language In Use Pre-Intermediate p.36
- Reward Pre-Intermediate pp.4-5,18-19
- The New Cambridge English Course 2 p.98
- True To Life Pre-Intermediate p.135

Early/Mid-Intermediate
- Intermediate Matters pp.22, 28
- Language In Use Intermediate p.17
- Meanings Into Words Intermediate pp.30-32
- New Headway Intermediate pp.98-99
- Survival Lessons pp.29,84-85
- Think Ahead to First Certificate pp.14,57

Upper Intermediate
- Headway Upper Intermediate pp.44-45,90
- Think First Certificate [Revised] pp.48,52

The Index: Grammar

TIME EXPRESSIONS contd.

Advanced
- English Vocabulary In Use pp.40-41
- Focus On Advanced English p.19
- Headway Advanced p.93

Various
- More Grammar Games pp.156-157

PERFECT ASPECT

Advanced
- Distinction pp.41-42
- Headway Advanced p.60
- Proficiency Masterclass pp.134-135

CONTINUOUS/PROGRESSIVE ASPECT

Advanced
- Distinction p.12
- Language Issues p.19
- Proficiency Masterclass pp.17-18

Various
- More Grammar Games pp.26-27

STATIVE VERBS

Pre-Intermediate
- Look Ahead 2 p.13

Early/Mid-Intermediate
- English Grammar In Use pp.8-9
- New Headway Intermediate pp.18-19
- Survival Lessons pp.21,68-69

Advanced
- Focus On Proficiency p.26
- Proficiency Masterclass p.19

TENSE MIX

Early/Mid-Intermediate
- English Grammar In Use p.276
- The New Cambridge English Course 3 pp.8-9
- Think Ahead to First Certificate p.12
- Workout Intermediate p.95

Upper Intermediate
- Headway Upper Intermediate p.8
- Upper Intermediate Matters pp.6,9

Advanced
- Focus On Advanced English p.25
- Headway Advanced pp.10,59,93
- Language Issues p.10
- Workout Advanced p.26 [Past tenses]

HAVE GOT

Beginner/Elementary
- Blueprint One pp.21-22
- Essential Grammar In Use pp.28-29
- Headway Elementary pp.70-71
- Look Ahead 1 pp.37-38
- Play Games With English 1 pp.28-29
- Streamline Departures Units 16-17
- The New Cambridge English Course 1 pp.16-17
- True To Life Elementary pp.13-17

Pre-Intermediate
- Headway Pre-Intermediate pp.13-15
- Language In Use Pre-Intermediate p.8
- Reward Pre-Intermediate pp.22-23

Early/Mid-Intermediate
- English Grammar In Use pp.34-35

Various
- Grammar Practice Activities pp.122-126

USED TO/WOULD/BE USED TO

Beginner/Elementary
- Play Games With English 2 pp.62-63 [used to]

Pre-Intermediate
- Blueprint Two pp.99-100 [used to]
- Headway Pre-Intermediate pp.71-72
- Pre-Intermediate Matters pp.86-87
- Streamline Connections Units 34,36 [used to]
- The New Cambridge English Course 2 pp.46-47
- The Pre-Intermediate Choice p.15 [used to]
- True To Life Pre-Intermediate pp.135-136

USED TO/WOULD/BE USED TO contd.

Early/Mid-Intermediate
- English Grammar In Use pp.36-37,120-121
- Intermediate Communication Games No.24 [used to]
- Intermediate Matters p.22 [Past Simple v. used to]
- Language In Use Intermediate pp.34-35
- Look Ahead Intermediate pp.8-9 [used to]
- Meanings Into Words Intermediate pp.67-74 [used to]
- New Blueprint Intermediate pp.28-29
- Survival Lessons pp.10,46-47
- The Intermediate Choice pp.28 [used to],43 [be v. get used to]
- Think Ahead to First Certificate p.21
- True To Life Intermediate pp.70-71 [used to],150-152
- Workout Intermediate p.59 [used to]

Upper Intermediate
- English Grammar Lessons pp.24-27
- First Certificate Gold p.82
- Headway Upper Intermediate pp.89-90
- Look Ahead Upper Intermediate pp.96-97,120-121
- Meanings Into Words Upper Intermediate pp.4-5
- New First Certificate Masterclass pp.12-13,17
- Think First Certificate [Revised] pp.75,130
- Upper Intermediate Matters p.11 [used to v. would],14 [be v. get used to]
- Workout Upper Intermediate p.39 [would v. used to]

Advanced
- Language Issues pp.24-27
- Proficiency Masterclass pp.161-162
- The Nelson Proficiency Course pp.191-192

Various
- Grammar Practice Activities pp.281-282 [used to]

CAN/COULD/ABLE TO

Beginner/Elementary
- Elementary Communication Games No.29
- Essential Grammar In Use pp.50-51
- Blueprint One pp.19-20
- The New Cambridge English Course 1 pp.64-65 [can/can't]
- Look Ahead 1 pp.74-75
- Streamline Departures Units 14 [can/can't],57 [can/could]
- The Beginners' Choice p.55 [can/can't]
- Headway Elementary pp.40-41 [can/could]
- True To Life Elementary pp.43-46

Pre-Intermediate
- Look Ahead 2 p.21 [could]
- Pre-Intermediate Matters pp.26-27 [can - possibility]
- Streamline Connections Units 16-17,24 [able to]
- Reward Pre-Intermediate pp.64-65

Early/Mid-Intermediate
- English Grammar In Use pp.52-53
- Headway Intermediate pp.54-55
- Intermediate Communication Games No.19
- Look Ahead Intermediate pp.80-81 [be able to, manage to],82-83 [can/could]
- New Blueprint Intermediate pp.42-43
- Survival Lessons pp.12,50-51
- The Intermediate Choice pp.84-85
- Workout Intermediate pp.70-71 [can, may]

Upper Intermediate
- First Certificate Gold p.86 [can, could, may, might]
- New First Certificate Masterclass pp.174-175
- Think First Certificate [Revised] p.42

Advanced
- Focus On Advanced English p.82
- Language Issues p.71
- Proficiency Masterclass p.45 [could, was able to, managed to]

Various
- Grammar Practice Activities p.172 [can/can't]

MUST (HAVE)/MIGHT (HAVE)/MAY (HAVE)CAN'T (HAVE)

Beginner/Elementary
- Essential Grammar In Use pp.52-53 [may/might]
- Play Games With English 2 pp.56-57

Pre-Intermediate
- Blueprint Two pp.73-74
- Headway Pre-Intermediate pp.95-96 [might]
- Reward Pre-Intermediate pp.86-87 [may/might]
- Streamline Connections Unit 73 [must be/can't be/may be]

MUST (HAVE)/MIGHT (HAVE)/MAY (HAVE)CAN'T (HAVE) contd.

- The New Cambridge English Course 2 pp.84-85
- The Pre-Intermediate Choice pp.54-55 [must be/might be/can't be]

Early/Mid-Intermediate
- English Grammar In Use pp.56-61
- Headway Intermediate pp.65-66 [might, could]
- Intermediate Communication Games No.30
- Look Ahead Intermediate p.75
- New Blueprint Intermediate pp.94-95
- New Headway Intermediate pp.86-90
- Play Games With English 3 pp.72-73
- The Intermediate Choice pp.26 [must/might/can't + verb],116 [must have/might have/can't have done]
- Think Ahead to First Certificate p.113

Upper Intermediate
- Blueprint Upper Intermediate pp.98-99
- English Grammar Lessons pp.80-83
- Look Ahead Upper Intermediate pp.104-105
- Meanings Into Words Upper Intermediate pp.63-65
- New First Certificate Masterclass pp.148-149
- Think First Certificate [Revised] p.95
- Upper Intermediate Matters p.115 [must/might/can't be],136-141 [must/might/can't have]
- Workout Upper Intermediate p.109 [must have/might have/can't have done]

Advanced
- Advanced Communication Games No.22
- Distinction pp.91-92,94
- Language Issues pp.71-73
- Proficiency Masterclass pp.47-48

Various
- Grammar Games pp.74-76

MUST/HAVE TO/NEED TO/DON'T HAVE TO

Beginner/Elementary
- Blueprint One pp.119-120
- Essential Grammar In Use pp.54-55,58-59
- Play Games With English 1 pp.56-57 [have got to]
- Streamline Departures Units 58 [must/need],69 [have/had to, don't/didn't have to]
- The Beginners' Choice p.109 [have to]
- True To Life Elementary pp.114-115,130-133 [need]

Pre-Intermediate
- Blueprint Two pp.21-22
- Headway Pre-Intermediate pp.56-59
- Language In Use Pre-Intermediate pp.76-77
- Look Ahead 2 pp.38-41
- Pre-Intermediate Matters pp.26-27
- Reward Pre-Intermediate pp.62-63 [must/mustn't]
- Streamline Connections Unit 15 [will have to]
- True To Life Pre-Intermediate pp.58-59,99-100
- Workout Pre-Intermediate pp.78-80

Early/Mid-Intermediate
- English Grammar In Use pp.62-65
- Headway Intermediate pp.42-44 [must, have to, should]
- Intermediate Communication Games No.39 [must/have to]
- Intermediate Matters pp.99-100
- Language In Use Intermediate p.24
- Look Ahead Intermediate p.25
- Meanings Into Words Intermediate pp.128-129
- New Blueprint Intermediate pp.70-71
- New Headway Intermediate pp.35-39
- Survival Lessons pp.13,52-53,14,54-55
- The Intermediate Choice pp.54-55

Upper Intermediate
- Blueprint Upper Intermediate p.33
- English Grammar Lessons pp.36-39
- First Certificate Gold p.124
- Look Ahead Upper Intermediate p.17
- New First Certificate Masterclass pp.134-135
- Think First Certificate [Revised] p.62
- Upper Intermediate Matters p.42 [obligation overview]
- Workout Upper Intermediate p.45 [must, have to, need to]

Advanced
- The Nelson Proficiency Course p.87

SHOULD/ (HAVE)/OUGHT TO (HAVE)

Beginner/Elementary
- Essential Grammar In Use pp.56-57
- Play Games With English 2 pp.34-35
- The Beginners' Choice pp.87-88 [should]
- True To Life Elementary pp.113-115 [should]

Pre-Intermediate
- Blueprint Two pp.53-54
- Headway Pre-Intermediate pp.58-59 [should/have to/don't have to]
- Language In Use Pre-Intermediate p.78

SHOULD/ (HAVE)/OUGHT TO (HAVE) contd.

- Look Ahead 2 p.65
- Pre-Intermediate Matters p.27
- Reward Pre-Intermediate pp.68-69
- Streamline Connections Unit 38 [should]
- The Pre-Intermediate Choice pp.24 [should/have to/don't have to],85 [should/shouldn't/have to/don't have to],87 [shouldn't/mustn't/don't have to]
- True To Life Pre-Intermediate pp.58-59

Early/Mid-Intermediate
- English Grammar In Use pp.66-69
- Intermediate Communication Games No.15
- Look Ahead Intermediate pp.50-51
- Meanings Into Words Intermediate pp.165-166, 168-170
- New Blueprint Intermediate pp.88-89
- New Headway Intermediate pp.37-38
- Play Games With English 3 pp.70-71 [should have]
- The Intermediate Choice p.96 [should have done]
- True To Life Intermediate pp.132,143-145
- Workout Intermediate p.83 [should/ought to/have to]

Upper Intermediate
- Blueprint Upper Intermediate p.33
- Headway Upper Intermediate p.97 [should have]
- Look Ahead Upper Intermediate p.25
- Meanings Into Words Upper Intermediate pp.97-98
- Upper Intermediate Matters pp.88-89

Advanced
- Proficiency Masterclass p.48 [need + should]
- The Nelson Proficiency Course p.86

MODALS (OVERVIEW)

Early/Mid-Intermediate
- English Grammar In Use p.278
- Intermediate Matters pp.98-100

Upper Intermediate
- First Certificate Gold p.116
- Headway Upper Intermediate pp.55,81-82
- Upper Intermediate Matters p.116

Advanced
- Focus On Advanced English pp.82,173
- Focus On Proficiency pp.62-63,162-164
- Headway Advanced pp.50-51
- Proficiency Masterclass pp.46-49
- Progress To Proficiency (New Edition) p.117
- The Nelson Proficiency Course pp.86-88
- Workout Advanced p.82

Various
- Grammar Practice Activities pp.172-180

CONDITIONALS

Beginner/Elementary
- Essential Grammar In Use pp.210-211
- Play Games With English 2 pp.74-75 [1st],80-81 [2nd]
- The New Cambridge English Course 1 p.113 [1st]

Pre-Intermediate
- Blueprint Two pp.103-104 [1st]
- Headway Pre-Intermediate pp.65-67 [1st], pp.93-94 [2nd]
- Language In Use Pre-Intermediate p.95 [1st]
- Look Ahead 2 pp.110-111 [1st]
- Pre-Intermediate Matters pp.57 [1st], 74-75 [2nd]
- Reward Pre-Intermediate pp.88-89 [1st],92-93 [2nd]
- Streamline Connections Units 56 [1st],69 [1st v. 2nd],71-72 [2nd]
- The New Cambridge English Course 2 pp.66-67 [1st],70-71 [2nd],104-105 [3rd]
- The Pre-Intermediate Choice pp.50 [1st],111 [2nd]
- True To Life Pre-Intermediate pp.105-106 [1st],122-123 [2nd]
- Workout Pre-Intermediate pp.94-95 [1st]

Early/Mid-Intermediate
- English Grammar In Use pp.74-79
- Headway Intermediate pp.48-51 [1st, 2nd, Zero]
- Intermediate Communication Games No.16 [2nd]
- Intermediate Matters pp.63-66 [1st],85-86 [2nd]
- Language In Use Intermediate pp.42-43 [2nd],102-103 [Past Conditionals]
- Look Ahead Intermediate pp.48-49 [1st and 2nd],120-121
- Meanings Into Words Intermediate pp.137 [1st],166 [2nd], 167-168 [3rd]

CONDITIONALS contd.

- New Blueprint Intermediate pp.46-47 [1st],82-83 [2nd],116-117 [3rd]
- New Headway Intermediate pp.76-79
- Play Games With English 3 pp.82-83 [3rd]
- Survival Lessons pp.15,56-57 [1st and 2nd],16,58-59 [3rd],17,60-61 [mixed]
- The Intermediate Choice pp.22 [1st],69 [2nd]
- The New Cambridge English Course 3 pp.126-127
- Think Ahead to First Certificate p.73 [1st and 2nd]
- True To Life Intermediate pp.87-88 [2nd],145-146 [3rd]
- Workout Intermediate pp.70-71 [Zero],75 [1st],86-7 [2nd]

Upper Intermediate
- Blueprint Upper Intermediate pp.68-69,72-73
- English Grammar Lessons pp.84-87
- First Certificate Gold pp.133-134 [Overview]
- Headway Upper Intermediate pp.97-98 [3rd]
- Look Ahead Upper Intermediate pp.56 [1st and 2nd],58-59 [3rd],80-81 [Zero, 1st, 2nd and 3rd]
- Meanings Into Words Upper Intermediate pp.66,79
- New First Certificate Masterclass pp.80 [Zero, 1st, 2nd],86 [3rd]
- The New Cambridge English Course 4 p.40 [3rd]
- Think First Certificate [Revised] p.143
- Upper Intermediate Matters pp.69-74 [Zero, First and Second],87-88 [3rd]
- Workout Upper Intermediate pp.53 [Zero],59 [1st],67 [2nd]

Advanced
- Advanced Communication Games No.32 [2nd]
- Distinction pp.101-102
- Focus On Advanced English pp.37-38 [1st and 2nd],148-149 [3rd and mixed]
- Focus On Proficiency pp.44-45 [1st and 2nd]
- Headway Advanced pp.82-83
- Language Issues pp.119-120
- Proficiency Masterclass pp.120-122
- Progress To Proficiency (New Edition) pp.148-149,201
- The Nelson Proficiency Course pp.109-111
- Workout Advanced p.63

Various
- Grammar Games pp.61-62 [1st],66-67 [1st]
- Grammar Practice Activities pp.75-82
- Keep Talking Activity No.39 [2nd]
- More Grammar Games pp.113-114,142,159-161 [2nd]

WISH etc.

Early/Mid-Intermediate
- English Grammar In Use pp.76-81
- Intermediate Communication Games No.3
- Intermediate Matters p.86
- Language In Use Intermediate pp.44,104
- New Blueprint Intermediate pp.114-115
- Play Games With English 3 pp.80-81
- Survival Lessons pp.34,94-95
- Think Ahead to First Certificate p.85
- True To Life Intermediate pp.110-112

Upper Intermediate
- Blueprint Upper Intermediate p.73
- First Certificate Gold pp.151-152
- Headway Upper Intermediate pp.93-94,97
- Look Ahead Upper Intermediate pp.48-49
- Meanings Into Words Upper Intermediate pp.94-102
- New First Certificate Masterclass p.154
- The New Cambridge English Course 4 pp.76-77
- Think First Certificate [Revised] p.145
- Upper Intermediate Matters pp.80-81,87-88
- Workout Upper Intermediate p.81

Advanced
- Advanced Communication Games Nos.20-21
- Distinction p.145
- Focus On Proficiency pp.79-80
- Headway Advanced pp.122-123
- Language Issues p.127
- Proficiency Masterclass pp.63-64
- Progress To Proficiency (New Edition) p.155
- Workout Advanced p.47

Various
- Grammar Games pp.112-114

PARTICIPLES

Advanced
- Language Issues pp.54-56
- Progress To Proficiency (New Edition) pp.15-17
- Workout Advanced p.106

PASSIVES

Beginner/Elementary
- Essential Grammar In Use pp.40-41
- Play Games With English 2 pp.40-41 [Past Simple passive],82-83 [Present Perfect Simple passive]

PASSIVES contd.

TO HAVE/GET SOMETHING DONE

REPORTED/DIRECT SPEECH

Beginner/Elementary
- Essential Grammar In Use pp.98-99

Pre-Intermediate
- Blueprint Two pp.75-76,115-116,119-120
- Headway Pre-Intermediate pp.112-114
- Look Ahead 2 pp.97-99
- Pre-Intermediate Matters pp.110-111
- Streamline Connections Units 35,74-76,79
- The Pre-Intermediate Choice p.115

Early/Mid-Intermediate
- English Grammar In Use pp.92-95
- Headway Intermediate pp.77-81
- Intermediate Communication Games No.31
- Intermediate Matters pp.113-114
- Language In Use Intermediate pp.77,95 [reported questions]
- Look Ahead Intermediate pp.112-113
- New Blueprint Intermediate pp.104-105,108-109
- New Headway Intermediate pp.116-119
- Play Games With English 3 pp.58-59,78-79
- The Intermediate Choice pp.48-49,69
- The New Cambridge English Course 3 pp.124-125
- Think Ahead to First Certificate pp.54-55,105 [reporting verbs]
- True To Life Intermediate pp.121-124

Upper Intermediate
- Blueprint Upper Intermediate pp.54-55
- English Grammar Lessons pp.120-123
- First Certificate Gold p.49
- Headway Upper Intermediate pp.80-81
- Look Ahead Upper Intermediate pp.74-75
- Meanings Into Words Upper Intermediate pp.52-59,89-90 [reported questions]
- New First Certificate Masterclass pp.108-109
- Think First Certificate [Revised] pp.110-111
- Upper Intermediate Matters pp.35 [reported questions],123-125
- Workout Upper Intermediate pp.86-87,95,101

Advanced
- Distinction pp.86,88
- Focus On Advanced English p.87
- Focus On Proficiency pp.182-185
- Proficiency Masterclass pp.149-151
- Progress To Proficiency (New Edition) pp.38-39,140
- Test Your Vocabulary 4 p.27
- Workout Advanced pp.97-98

Various
- Grammar Practice Activities pp.136-142
- More Grammar Games p.90 [without 'backshift']

SHORT ANSWERS E.G. *SO AM I/SO DO I* etc.

Beginner/Elementary
- Essential Grammar In Use pp.78-79
- Play Games With English 2 pp.48-49

Pre-Intermediate
- Streamline Connections Unit 31
- The New Cambridge English Course 2 pp.30-31
- True To Life Pre-Intermediate pp.127-128

Early/Mid-Intermediate
- Look Ahead Intermediate p.19
- Meanings Into Words Intermediate pp.121-122
- New Headway Intermediate p.95

Upper Intermediate
- Headway Upper Intermediate pp.28,65
- Think First Certificate [Revised] p.23

-ING v. INFINITIVE

Beginner/Elementary
- Essential Grammar In Use pp.94-95
- Headway Elementary pp.106-107

Pre-Intermediate
- Headway Pre-Intermediate pp.33-34
- Pre-Intermediate Matters pp.50-51
- True To Life Pre-Intermediate pp.63-65

Early/Mid-Intermediate
- English Grammar In Use pp.104-115
- Intermediate Matters p.120
- New Headway Intermediate pp.58-59
- Play Games With English 3 pp.74-75
- Survival Lessons pp.18,62-63
- The Intermediate Choice p.103
- The New Cambridge English Course 3 pp.16-17
- Think Ahead to First Certificate p.27
- True To Life Intermediate pp.20-22

-ING v. INFINITIVE contd.

Upper Intermediate
- Blueprint Upper Intermediate p.113
- English Grammar Lessons pp.104-107,116-119
- First Certificate Gold p.66
- Headway Upper Intermediate pp.26-28
- Look Ahead Upper Intermediate p.89
- New First Certificate Masterclass pp.38-39
  [gerunds],43
- Think First Certificate [Revised] p.164
- Upper Intermediate Matters pp.100-101

Advanced
- Distinction pp.55,58
- Focus On Advanced English pp.32-33 [*-ing* forms],207
- Focus On Proficiency pp.97-99,102-103,109-110
- Language Issues p.56
- Proficiency Masterclass pp.163-164
- Progress To Proficiency (New Edition) pp.54-55
- The Nelson Proficiency Course pp.149-151,169-170
- Workout Advanced p.40

Various
- More Grammar Games pp.1-4,62-63,68

INFINITIVE OF PURPOSE

Beginner/Elementary
- Blueprint One pp.107-108
- Essential Grammar In Use pp.100-101
- Headway Elementary pp.84-85
- Play Games With English 2 pp.36-37

Early/Mid-Intermediate
- English Grammar In Use pp.126-127
- Intermediate Matters p.42

Various
- Grammar Practice Activities pp.279-280

SOME v. ANY

Beginner/Elementary
- Blueprint One pp.53-54
- Essential Grammar In Use pp.140-141
- Headway Elementary pp.35-36
- Look Ahead 1 pp.32-33
- Streamline Departures Unit 10
- The New Cambridge English Course 1 p.34

Pre-Intermediate
- Language In Use Pre-Intermediate p.42
- Pre-Intermediate Matters p.38
- Reward Pre-Intermediate pp.34-35

Early/Mid-Intermediate
- English Grammar In Use pp.168-169

SOME, ANY, NO, EVERY

Beginner/Elementary
- Essential Grammar In Use pp.146-149

Pre-Intermediate
- Look Ahead 2 p.73
- Pre-Intermediate Matters p.92

COUNTABLE v. UNCOUNTABLE NOUNS *(+ much/many etc.)*

Beginner/Elementary
- Blueprint One pp.53-54
- Essential Grammar In Use pp.122-125,154-157
- Headway Elementary pp.64-65
- Look Ahead 1 pp.32-33,57,97
- Play Games With English 2 pp.70-71
- Streamline Departures Units 17,49
- The Beginners' Choice p.73
- The New Cambridge English Course 1 pp.32,34-35
- True To Life Elementary p.21

Pre-Intermediate
- Blueprint Two pp.51-52
- Headway Pre-Intermediate pp.26-28
- Language In Use Pre-Intermediate pp.42-44
- Pre-Intermediate Matters pp.38-39
  [much/many/a lot of/a few/a little]
- Reward Pre-Intermediate pp.34-35,78-79
- The Pre-Intermediate Choice p.96
  [much/many/a lot]
- True To Life Pre-Intermediate pp.85-86
- Workout Pre-Intermediate p.65

Early/Mid-Intermediate
- English Grammar In Use pp.136-141,172-173
- Intermediate Matters pp.106-107
- Play Games With English 3 pp.10-11
- Survival Lessons pp.30,86-87
- The Intermediate Choice pp.78-79
- Think Ahead to First Certificate pp.34-35
- True To Life Intermediate pp.16-17

COUNTABLE v. UNCOUNTABLE NOUNS (+ *much/many etc.*) contd.

Upper Intermediate
- A Way With Words 3 p.15
- First Certificate Gold p.88
- Headway Upper Intermediate pp.54-55,108
- Upper Intermediate Matters p.107

Advanced
- English Vocabulary In Use pp.52-61
- Progress To Proficiency (New Edition) pp.22-24
- The Nelson Proficiency Course pp.10-11

Various
- Grammar Games pp.13-14
- Grammar Practice Activities pp.86-93

ARTICLES

Beginner/Elementary
- Essential Grammar In Use pp.118-119 [a/an],126-129,134-135 [the]
- Headway Elementary pp.27-28
- The Beginners' Choice p.102

Pre-Intermediate
- Headway Pre-Intermediate p.28
- Pre-Intermediate Matters pp.44 [the],74 [the]
- Reward Pre-Intermediate pp.6-7
- True To Life Pre-Intermediate pp.97-98

Early/Mid-Intermediate
- English Grammar In Use pp.142-155
- Intermediate Matters p.8
- Look Ahead Intermediate pp.90-91
- Survival Lessons pp.31,88-89
- The Intermediate Choice p.80
- The New Cambridge English Course 3 p.125
- Think Ahead to First Certificate pp.96-97

Upper Intermediate
- Blueprint Upper Intermediate pp.17,94
- English Grammar Lessons pp.52-55
- First Certificate Gold pp.112-113
- Headway Upper Intermediate pp.107-108
- Look Ahead Upper Intermediate pp.34-35
- New First Certificate Masterclass p.24
- Think First Certificate [Revised] pp.84-85
- Upper Intermediate Matters pp.15,67

Advanced
- Distinction p.114
- Language Issues pp.31-32
- Progress To Proficiency (New Edition) pp.22-24
- Workout Advanced p.59

Various
- More Grammar Games pp.162-163
- Grammar Practice Activities pp.53-54

SINGULAR v. PLURAL

Beginner/Elementary
- The Beginners' Choice p.18
- The New Cambridge English Course 1 p.16

Pre-Intermediate
- Reward Pre-Intermediate pp.6-7
- True To Life Pre-Intermediate p.84

Early/Mid-Intermediate
- Elementary Vocabulary pp.56-57
- English Grammar In Use pp.156-157
- Essential Grammar In Use pp.120-121
- Start Testing Your Vocabulary p.21

Various
- Grammar Games pp.121-122

MODIFIERS/INTENSIFIERS

Pre-Intermediate
- The Pre-Intermediate Choice p.55

Early/Mid-Intermediate
- English Grammar In Use pp.206-207 [quite/rather]
- Headway Intermediate p.57

Upper Intermediate
- English Grammar Lessons pp.108-111
- First Certificate Gold p.122
- Think First Certificate [Revised] p.154

Advanced
- Language Issues pp.49-51
- Proficiency Masterclass p.75
- Progress To Proficiency (New Edition) pp.84-85,268-269

POSSESSIVE ADJECTIVES
(my,your,his,her etc.)

Beginner/Elementary
- Blueprint One pp.67-68
- Essential Grammar In Use pp.108-109
- Headway Elementary p.9
- The Beginners' Choice p.43

Pre-Intermediate
- Reward Pre-Intermediate pp.20-21

Various
- Grammar Practice Activities pp.228-229

POSSESSIVE PRONOUNS
(mine,yours,his,hers etc.)

Beginner/Elementary
- Blueprint One pp.67-68
- Essential Grammar In Use pp.110-111
- Headway Elementary p.79
- Streamline Departures Unit 18

Pre-Intermediate
- The Pre-Intermediate Choice p.27

Various
- Grammar Practice Activities pp.226-229

POSSESSIVE *'S*

Beginner/Elementary
- Essential Grammar In Use pp.116-117
- Headstart pp.18-20
- Play Games With English 1 pp.40-41
- Streamline Departures Unit 9
- The Beginners' Choice p.19
- The New Cambridge English Course 1 pp.15-16

Pre-Intermediate
- Reward Pre-Intermediate pp.20-21

Early/Mid-Intermediate
- English Grammar In Use pp.160-161
- Intermediate Matters p.49

Upper Intermediate
- English Grammar Lessons pp.132-135

Advanced
- Language Issues p.94

Various
- More Grammar Games p.89
- Grammar Practice Activities pp.226-228

QUESTION TAGS

Beginner/Elementary
- Play Games With English 2 pp.48-49

Pre-Intermediate
- Blueprint Two pp.83-84
- Headway Pre-Intermediate p.76
- Look Ahead 2 pp.66-67
- Pre-Intermediate Matters p.87
- Streamline Connections Units 22,28
- The New Cambridge English Course 2 pp.102-103

Early/Mid-Intermediate
- English Grammar In Use pp.102-103
- Intermediate Matters pp.28-29
- Language In Use Intermediate p.96
- New Headway Intermediate pp.109-110
- Survival Lessons pp.32,90-91
- The Intermediate Choice p.117
- The New Cambridge English Course 3 p.38

Upper Intermediate
- Blueprint Upper Intermediate p.13
- English Grammar Lessons pp.28-31
- Headway Upper Intermediate p.38
- Look Ahead Upper Intermediate p.27
- Meanings Into Words Upper Intermediate pp.88-89
- New First Certificate Masterclass p.179

Advanced
- Language Issues pp.139-140
- Progress To Proficiency (New Edition) p.132
- Workout Advanced p.72

Various
- Grammar Games pp.22-27
- Grammar Practice Activities pp.275-277

INDIRECT (EMBEDDED) QUESTIONS

Beginner/Elementary
- Essential Grammar In Use pp.92-93

Pre-Intermediate
- Look Ahead 2 pp.58-59
- True To Life Pre-Intermediate pp.20-22

INDIRECT (EMBEDDED) QUESTIONS contd.

Early/Mid-Intermediate
- English Grammar In Use pp.98-99
- Intermediate Matters p.9
- Language In Use Intermediate p.95
- Look Ahead Intermediate p.123
- New Headway Intermediate pp.107-108
- Think Ahead to First Certificate p.41

Upper Intermediate
- Blueprint Upper Intermediate p.29
- Headway Upper Intermediate pp.37-38
- Meanings Into Words Upper Intermediate p.86
- Upper Intermediate Matters p.35

INVERSION

Beginner/Elementary
- The Beginners' Choice p.20 [inverted questions]

Upper Intermediate
- Blueprint Upper Intermediate p.111
- Look Ahead Upper Intermediate pp.114-115
- Think First Certificate [Revised] p.153

Advanced
- Distinction p.66
- Focus On Proficiency pp.40-41
- Headway Advanced pp.112-113
- Proficiency Masterclass pp.177-178
- Progress To Proficiency (New Edition) p.45
- The Nelson Proficiency Course pp.30-31
- Workout Advanced p.66 [not only, hardly etc.]

SUBJECT v. OBJECT QUESTIONS

Beginner/Elementary
- Essential Grammar In Use pp.84-85
- Streamline Departures Unit 30

Pre-Intermediate
- Headway Pre-Intermediate p.73
- The Pre-Intermediate Choice p.78

Early/Mid-Intermediate
- English Grammar In Use pp.96-97
- Language In Use Intermediate p.17
- Think Ahead to First Certificate p.123

Upper Intermediate
- Look Ahead Upper Intermediate pp.72-73
- Upper Intermediate Matters p.34

QUESTIONS (OVERVIEW)

Beginner/Elementary
- Essential Grammar In Use pp.82-93
- Headway Elementary pp.92-93

Pre-Intermediate
- Headway Pre-Intermediate pp.7-8
- Pre-Intermediate Matters pp.8-9
- Streamline Connections Unit 51
- The Pre-Intermediate Choice pp.6,10
- True To Life Pre-Intermediate pp.12-16

Early/Mid-Intermediate
- English Grammar In Use pp.96-99
- Intermediate Communication Games No.10
- Language In Use Intermediate pp.94-96

Upper Intermediate
- English Grammar Lessons pp.28-31
- First Certificate Gold pp.9-10
- Headway Upper Intermediate pp.30,36-38
- Meanings Into Words Upper Intermediate pp.85-90
- Upper Intermediate Matters p.34
- Workout Upper Intermediate p.17

Various
- More Grammar Games pp.60,94-96,98-99
- Grammar Practice Activities pp.148-164
- The Q Book pp.40-41

OBJECT PRONOUNS
(me,you,him,her etc.)

Beginner/Elementary
- Blueprint One pp.25-26
- Look Ahead 1 p.75
- The Beginners' Choice p.67
- The New Cambridge English Course 1 p.28

REFLEXIVE PRONOUNS
(myself,yourself,himself,herself etc.)

Beginner/Elementary
- Essential Grammar In Use pp.114-15

Pre-Intermediate
- Streamline Connections Unit 26
- The New Cambridge English Course 2 pp.90-91
- True To Life Pre-Intermediate pp.33-34

Early/Mid-Intermediate
- English Grammar In Use pp.164-165
- Look Ahead Intermediate pp.34-35
- Play Games With English 3 pp.40-41

Upper Intermediate
- Blueprint Upper Intermediate p.111

Advanced
- Headway Advanced p.31

RELATIVE CLAUSES
(DEFINING/NON-DEFINING)

Beginner/Elementary
- Essential Grammar In Use pp.212-215

Pre-Intermediate
- Blueprint Two pp.11-12,87-88
- Pre-Intermediate Matters pp.80-81
- Reward Pre-Intermediate pp.56-57
- Streamline Connections Units 41,44
- The Pre-Intermediate Choice p.95
- True To Life Pre-Intermediate p.141

Early/Mid-Intermediate
- English Grammar In Use pp.182-89
- Intermediate Matters p.42
- Look Ahead Intermediate pp.56-57
- Meanings Into Words Intermediate pp.5,144-145
- Play Games With English 3 pp.76-77
- The Intermediate Choice p.29

Upper Intermediate
- English Grammar Lessons pp.60-63
- First Certificate Gold pp.99-100
- Headway Upper Intermediate pp.73-74
- Look Ahead Upper Intermediate pp.106-107
- Meanings Into Words Upper Intermediate pp.25-27

- New First Certificate Masterclass pp.94-95
- The New Cambridge English Course 4 pp.62-63
- Think First Certificate [Revised] pp.148-149
- Upper Intermediate Matters pp.130-131

Advanced
- Distinction pp.77,79
- Focus On Advanced English pp.11 [reduced relative clauses],132
- Focus On Proficiency pp.117-118
- Headway Advanced p.102
- Language Issues pp.103-104
- Proficiency Masterclass p.5
- Progress To Proficiency (New Edition) p.243
- Workout Advanced pp.76-77

Various
- Grammar Practice Activities pp.268-272

RELATIVE PRONOUNS

Beginner/Elementary
- Play Games With English 2 pp.68-69

Early/Mid-Intermediate
- English Grammar In Use pp.182-189
- New Blueprint Intermediate pp.72-73
- New Headway Intermediate p.64
- Play Games With English 3 pp.34-35
- Think Ahead to First Certificate p.22

Upper Intermediate
- First Certificate Gold pp.99-100

Advanced
- Focus On Advanced English p.21
- Language Issues p.104
- The Nelson Proficiency Course pp.192-194

DEMONSTRATIVE PRONOUNS
(this,that,these,those)

Beginner/Elementary
- Essential Grammar In Use pp.136-137
- Look Ahead 1 p.47
- Play Games With English 1 pp.8-9
- Play Games With English 2 pp.8-9
- The New Cambridge English Course 1 p.50

Upper Intermediate
- The New Cambridge English Course 4 p.99

ADJECTIVES (-*ING* v. -*ED*)

Pre-Intermediate
- Headway Pre-Intermediate p.90
- Pre-Intermediate Matters p.46
- Streamline Connections Unit 37
- The Pre-Intermediate Choice pp.42-43

Early/Mid-Intermediate
- English Grammar In Use pp.194-195
- Headway Intermediate p.27
- Intermediate Matters p.43
- Play Games With English 3 pp.28-29
- Survival Lessons pp.24,74-75

Upper Intermediate
- First Certificate Gold p.7
- Workout Upper Intermediate p.23

ADJECTIVE ORDER

Pre-Intermediate
- Pre-Intermediate Matters p.81
- Workout Pre-Intermediate p.30

Early/Mid-Intermediate
- English Grammar In Use pp.196-197
- Intermediate Matters p.49
- Survival Lessons pp.25,76-77
- The Intermediate Choice p.15
- Think Ahead to First Certificate p.42

Upper Intermediate
- Look Ahead Upper Intermediate pp.82-83
- Think First Certificate [Revised] p.135

Advanced
- Distinction p.127
- Headway Advanced p.71
- Language Issues pp.47-48
- Workout Advanced pp.35-36

SO/SUCH

Pre-Intermediate
- Blueprint Two pp.101-102
- The Pre-Intermediate Choice p.102
- True To Life Pre-Intermediate p.38

Early/Mid-Intermediate
- English Grammar In Use pp.202-203
- Meanings Into Words Intermediate pp.153-155
- Think Ahead to First Certificate p.19

ADVERBS

Beginner/Elementary
- Blueprint One pp.117-118
- Essential Grammar In Use pp.160-161
- Headway Elementary p.94
- Play Games With English 2 pp.26-27
- Streamline Departures Units 38,50
- The Beginners' Choice p.111 [manner]
- The New Cambridge English Course 1 p.111
- True To Life Elementary pp.106-108

Pre-Intermediate
- Headway Pre-Intermediate pp.54,90
- Look Ahead 2 p.53
- Pre-Intermediate Matters p.56
- True To Life Pre-Intermediate pp.145-146

Early/Mid-Intermediate
- English Grammar In Use pp.198-201
- Intermediate Communication Games No.37
- Intermediate Matters p.50
- Play Games With English 3 pp.18-19
- Survival Lessons pp.26,78-79 [position in a sentence]
- The New Cambridge English Course 3 p.104 [position in a sentence]
- Think Ahead to First Certificate pp.66-67

Upper Intermediate
- English Grammar Lessons pp.92-95,124-127
- Look Ahead Upper Intermediate p.51
- New First Certificate Masterclass p.140

Advanced
- Headway Advanced pp.71-73,108-109
- Language Issues pp.45-46 [word order]
- Progress To Proficiency (New Edition) pp.31-33 [position in a sentence]

Various
- Grammar Practice Activities pp.48-52
- Keep Talking Activity No.106

TOO/ENOUGH/VERY

Beginner/Elementary
- Essential Grammar In Use pp.170-173
- Streamline Departures Unit 64
- The Beginners' Choice p.111 [too v. very]
- The New Cambridge English Course 1 p.35
- True To Life Elementary p.40

TOO/ENOUGH/VERY contd.

Pre-Intermediate
- Language In Use Pre-Intermediate pp.43-44 [too/enough]
- Look Ahead 2 p.33
- Pre-Intermediate Matters p.93 [too v. very]
- Reward Pre-Intermediate pp.78-79
- Streamline Connections Units 13,49
- True To Life Pre-Intermediate pp.71-72

Early/Mid-Intermediate
- English Grammar In Use pp.204-205
- Intermediate Matters p.59 [very/too/not enough]
- Language In Use Intermediate p.61 [too/enough]
- Meanings Into Words Intermediate pp.151-153
- The Intermediate Choice p.108 [very/too/enough]

Upper Intermediate
- New First Certificate Masterclass p.140
- Think First Certificate [Revised] p.121

COMPARATIVES/SUPERLATIVES etc.

Beginner/Elementary
- Blueprint One pp.87-90
- Conversation Pieces pp.37-40,53-56
- Essential Grammar In Use pp.162-169
- Headway Elementary pp.69-73
- Play Games With English 1 pp.48-51
- Play Games With English 2 pp.30-31
- Speaking Elementary [Oxford Supp. Skills] pp.22-23
- Streamline Departures Units 68,70-71
- The Beginners' Choice pp.85-86,95-97
- The New Cambridge English Course 1 pp.66-67
- True To Life Elementary pp.81-86

Pre-Intermediate
- Blueprint Two pp.89-90
- Headway Pre-Intermediate pp.41-43
- Language In Use Pre-Intermediate pp.60-62
- Look Ahead 2 pp.25,35
- Pre-Intermediate Matters pp.68-69
- Reward Pre-Intermediate pp.42-45
- Streamline Connections Units 20 [comparative adverbs],27 [as...as]
- The New Cambridge English Course 2 pp.18-19,30-33
- The Pre-Intermediate Choice pp.13,20-21,30
- True To Life Pre-Intermediate pp.43-44

Early/Mid-Intermediate
- English Grammar In Use pp.208-215
- Headway Intermediate pp.31-33
- Intermediate Communication Games No.32
- Intermediate Matters pp.58-59
- Language In Use Intermediate pp.60-61
- Meanings Into Words Intermediate pp.59-65
- The Intermediate Choice p.37
- The New Cambridge English Course 3 p.129
- Think Ahead to First Certificate p.64
- Workout Intermediate pp.14,15,26-7

Upper Intermediate
- Blueprint Upper Intermediate pp.89-90
- English Grammar Lessons pp.64-67
- First Certificate Gold pp.28-29
- Look Ahead Upper Intermediate pp.32-33
- Meanings Into Words Upper Intermediate pp.115-121
- New First Certificate Masterclass pp.52-53
- Think First Certificate [Revised] pp.120-121
- Upper Intermediate Matters p.52

Advanced
- Advanced Communication Games Nos.6,39
- Distinction pp.106-107
- Focus On Advanced English pp.63-64,73-74
- Language Issues pp.133-135
- Progress To Proficiency (New Edition) p.8
- Test Your Vocabulary 4 pp.56-57 [idioms of comparison]
- Workout Advanced p.90

Various
- Grammar Games p.118
- Grammar Practice Activities pp.62-74
- More Grammar Games pp.91,143-145
- The Q Book pp.16-17

WORD ORDER

Beginner/Elementary
- Essential Grammar In Use pp.174-177
- Play Games With English 1 pp.86-87
- Play Games With English 2 pp.64-65

Early/Mid-Intermediate
- English Grammar In Use pp.216-219
- Play Games With English 3 pp.42-43,56-57

Upper Intermediate
- A Way With Words 3 pp.6-8
- English Grammar Lessons pp.132-135
- First Certificate Gold p.103
- Think First Certificate [Revised] p.135
- Upper Intermediate Matters p.37

WORD ORDER contd.

Advanced
- Language Issues pp.45-48
- Progress To Proficiency (New Edition) pp.69-70 [position of adjectives and participles]

Various
- Grammar Games pp.64-65
- More Grammar Games pp.5-7,44-45,164-165

LIKE

Beginner/Elementary
- Headway Elementary pp.62-63
- Play Games With English 1 p.47
- Streamline Departures Units 11 [would like],29 [like/not like]
- The Beginners' Choice p.79

Pre-Intermediate
- Headway Pre-Intermediate pp.34,40-41

Early/Mid-Intermediate
- English Grammar In Use pp.232-233 [like v. as]
- Headway Intermediate pp.7-8,30-31
- Intermediate Matters p.48
- New Headway Intermediate pp.56-57
- The Intermediate Choice p.95
- Think Ahead to First Certificate p.79

Upper Intermediate
- First Certificate Gold p.39

Advanced
- Focus On Advanced English p.64
- Headway Advanced pp.40-41 [like v. as]
- Language Issues p.135 [like v. as]
- Workout Advanced p.114 [like v. as]

PREPOSITIONS (PLACE, TIME, DIRECTION)

Beginner/Elementary
- Blueprint One pp.55-56 [place]
- Elementary Communication Games Nos.6-7 [place]
- Essential Grammar In Use pp.182-183,188-197
- Headway Elementary p.35
- Look Ahead 1 pp.62-63 [time]
- Play Games With English 1 pp.24-25 [place],80-81 [time]
- Play Games With English 2 pp.18-19 [place]

- Start Testing Your Vocabulary pp.4-5 [place],25 [time]
- The Beginners' Choice pp.14 [time],41,54,75 [place]
- The New Cambridge English Course 1 pp.14 [place],75 [time]

Pre-Intermediate
- Language In Use Pre-Intermediate p.10 [place]
- Reward Pre-Intermediate pp.32-33 [place],38-39 [time and place]
- Test Your Vocabulary 1 p.25

Early/Mid-Intermediate
- English Grammar In Use pp.240-253 [on/in/at]
- Meanings Into Words Intermediate pp.2-3 [place],22-23 [direction],112-114 [location]
- Play Games With English 3 pp.20-21 [movement]
- Survival Lessons pp.27,80-81 [location],28,82-83 [time]
- Think Ahead to First Certificate pp.24-25 [position/direction]

Upper Intermediate
- English Grammar Lessons pp.16-19

Advanced
- Progress To Proficiency (New Edition) pp.224-225

Various
- Grammar Practice Activities pp.230-235
- More Grammar Games pp.32-33,92 [movement]

WORD AND PREPOSITION COMBINATIONS

Beginner/Elementary
- Essential Grammar In Use pp.198-201
- Start Testing Your Vocabulary pp.41,66

Pre-Intermediate
- Blueprint Two p.122
- Headway Pre-Intermediate p.24
- Streamline Connections Unit 32
- Test Your Vocabulary 1 pp.16,48
- True To Life Pre-Intermediate p.81

Early/Mid-Intermediate
- English Grammar In Use pp.122-123,256-271
- Intermediate Matters p.36
- Play Games With English 3 pp.30-31,48-49
- Test Your Vocabulary 2 pp.22,39
- Think Ahead to First Certificate pp.65,100

WORD AND PREPOSITION COMBINATIONS contd.

Upper Intermediate
- A Way With Words 3 pp.34-37
- English Grammar Lessons pp.112-115
- Test Your Vocabulary 3 pp.21,64
- Think First Certificate [Revised] pp.130,144
- Upper Intermediate Matters pp.27,122

Advanced
- Headway Advanced pp.45,82
- Progress To Proficiency (New Edition) pp.108,179-181,264-265
- Test Your Vocabulary 4 (Adv.) pp.20,45

CLEFT SENTENCES

Advanced
- Language Issues p.142
- Proficiency Masterclass p.106

MAKE/DO

Pre-Intermediate
- Headway Pre-Intermediate p.62
- Pre-Intermediate Matters p.112

Early/Mid-Intermediate
- Intermediate Matters p.127
- New Blueprint Intermediate p.64

Upper Intermediate
- First Certificate Gold p.100

Advanced
- Advanced Vocabulary and Idiom p.58
- English Vocabulary In Use pp.170-171
- Focus On Proficiency p.31
- Progress To Proficiency (New Edition) p.64
- Test Your Vocabulary 4 p.58

MAKE/LET/ALLOW

Pre-Intermediate
- Headway Pre-Intermediate pp.84-85 [make v. let]

Early/Mid-Intermediate
- Language In Use Intermediate p.25 [make v. let]
- Meanings Into Words Intermediate pp.130-131
- Think Ahead to First Certificate p.121 [make v. let]

Upper Intermediate
- First Certificate Gold p.144
- Look Ahead Upper Intermediate p.17
- The New Cambridge English Course 4 pp.52-53
- Upper Intermediate Matters p.44

THERE IS/ARE

Beginner/Elementary
- Blueprint One pp.41-42
- Essential Grammar In Use pp.62-65
- Headstart pp.51-53
- Headway Elementary pp.34-36
- Play Games With English 1 pp.20-21
- Play Games With English 2 pp.10-11
- Streamline Departures Unit 6
- The Beginners' Choice p.41
- The New Cambridge English Course 1 p.24

Pre-Intermediate
- Language In Use Pre-Intermediate p.8

Various
- Grammar Practice Activities pp.165-171

IT, THERE etc.

Beginner/Elementary
- Essential Grammar In Use pp.66-67

Early/Mid-Intermediate
- English Grammar In Use pp.166-167

Advanced
- Distinction p.128
- Language Issues pp.87-90
- Progress To Proficiency (New Edition) pp.123 [there],173 [it]

ALTHOUGH, IN SPITE OF etc.

Pre-Intermediate
- Blueprint Two p.92 [although, however]
- Reward Pre-Intermediate pp.82-83
- True To Life Pre-Intermediate pp.142-143

Early/Mid-Intermediate
- English Grammar In Use pp.224-225
- Meanings Into Words Intermediate p.175
- The Intermediate Choice p.87
- Think Ahead to First Certificate p.39 [despite, although]

Upper Intermediate
- Blueprint Upper Intermediate p.31
- Headway Upper Intermediate pp.62-63
- Look Ahead Upper Intermediate p.19
- Think First Certificate [Revised] p.119

Advanced
- Focus On Advanced English p.38
- Focus On Proficiency p.90
- Language Issues pp.79-81

Section 2: Functions

GIVING ADVICE

Beginner/Elementary
• Conversation Pieces pp.53-56

Pre-Intermediate
• Blueprint Two pp.53-54
• Look Ahead 2 p.81
• Reward Pre-Intermediate pp.68-69
• Streamline Connections Units 38,72
• The Pre-Intermediate Choice pp.116-7
• True To Life Pre-Intermediate p.110
• Workout Pre-Intermediate p.97

Early/Mid-Intermediate
• Intermediate Communication Games No.15
• Intermediate Matters p.88
• Language In Use Intermediate p.84
• Meanings Into Words Intermediate pp.98-102
• The Intermediate Choice p.94
• Think Ahead to First Certificate pp.46-47

Upper Intermediate
• English Grammar Lessons pp.72-75
• First Certificate Gold p.70
• Upper Intermediate Matters p.43
• Workout Upper Intermediate p.75

Advanced
• Advanced Communication Games No.37

Various
• More Grammar Games p.71

AGREEING/DISAGREEING

Beginner/Elementary
• The New Cambridge English Course 1 p.86

Pre-Intermediate
• The Pre-Intermediate Choice p.110

Early/Mid-Intermediate
• The Intermediate Choice p.23
• Think Ahead to First Certificate p.83

Upper Intermediate
• First Certificate Gold p.62
• Look Ahead Upper Intermediate pp.12-13
• Think First Certificate [Revised] p.90
• Upper Intermediate Matters p.15
• Workout Upper Intermediate p.103

Advanced
• Distinction p.52
• Workout Advanced p.27

MAKING APOLOGIES

Beginner/Elementary
• True To Life Elementary pp.125-128

Pre-Intermediate
• Pre-Intermediate Matters p.96

Early/Mid-Intermediate
• New Blueprint Intermediate pp.26-27

Advanced
• Advanced Communication Games No.33

REQUESTING CLARIFICATION

Early/Mid-Intermediate
• New Blueprint Intermediate pp.92-93
• Workout Intermediate p.78

Advanced
• Workout Advanced p.60

MAKING COMPLAINTS

Beginner/Elementary
• True To Life Elementary pp.124-126

Pre-Intermediate
• The Pre-Intermediate Choice pp.117-118
• Workout Pre-Intermediate p.29

Early/Mid-Intermediate
• New Blueprint Intermediate pp.62-63
• New Headway Intermediate p.106
• The Intermediate Choice pp.39-40
• The New Cambridge English Course 3 pp.58-59
• Think Ahead to First Certificate pp.10-11

Upper Intermediate
• First Certificate Gold pp.95-96

Advanced
• Advanced Communication Games No.24

The Index: *Functions*

MAKING COMPLAINTS contd.

Various
- The Q Book pp.30-31

DESCRIBING OBJECTS

Beginner/Elementary
- Elementary Communication Games No.13
- Elementary Vocabulary p.37 [materials]

Pre-Intermediate
- Look Ahead 2 pp.72-79
- Pre-Intermediate Matters p.81
- Reward Pre-Intermediate pp.58-59
- The New Cambridge English Course 2 pp.88-89
- Workout Pre-Intermediate pp.74-76

Early/Mid-Intermediate
- Intermediate Communication Games Nos.2,33
- Language In Use Intermediate pp.46-47
- Meanings Into Words Intermediate pp.143-149
- Think Ahead to First Certificate p.40
- Vocabulary Builder 1 pp.74-77

Upper Intermediate
- Headway Upper Intermediate p.72
- Look Ahead Upper Intermediate p.83
- Test Your Vocabulary 3 p.37 [objects]
- Think First Certificate [Revised] pp.134-135

Advanced
- Advanced Vocabulary and Idiom p.71
- Focus On Proficiency p.165
- Wordbuilder pp.114-118

DESCRIBING PEOPLE

Beginner/Elementary
- Blueprint One pp.73-74
- Conversation Pieces pp.5-8
- Elementary Communication Games No.14
- Elementary Task Listening pp.8-9
- Elementary Vocabulary pp.34-36
- Headway Elementary p.77
- Listening Elementary [Oxford Supp. Skills] pp.4-5
- Look Ahead 1 pp.48-49
- Play Games With English 1 pp.44-45
- Speaking Elementary [Oxford Supp. Skills] pp.6-7
- The Beginners' Choice pp.66-67
- The New Cambridge English Course 1 pp.15,44,69

- True To Life Elementary pp.37-41

Pre-Intermediate
- Blueprint Two pp.117-118
- Language In Use Pre-Intermediate pp.90-93
- Pre-Intermediate Matters pp.22,82
- Reward Pre-Intermediate pp.40-41
- Test Your Vocabulary 1 p.24
- The New Cambridge English Course 2 pp.86-87
- The Pre-Intermediate Choice pp.55-56
- Workout Pre-Intermediate pp.30-31,56-57

Early/Mid-Intermediate
- Headway Intermediate pp.13,30-31,33
- Intermediate Communication Games Nos.7,36
- Intermediate Matters pp.47-51
- Look Ahead Intermediate pp.72-77
- New Headway Intermediate pp.22-23
- Play Games With English 3 pp.38-39
- Task Listening pp.26,52-53
- Test Your Vocabulary 2 p.19
- The Intermediate Choice pp.29,108
- Think Ahead to First Certificate pp.61,78
- Workout Intermediate p.45

Upper Intermediate
- Blueprint Upper Intermediate pp.23-25,30-31
- First Certificate Gold pp.30,34,79,81
- Headway Upper Intermediate pp.67-70
- Look Ahead Upper Intermediate pp.84-85
- Meanings Into Words Upper Intermediate pp.10-16,158-159
- New First Certificate Masterclass pp.98-103
- Test Your Vocabulary 3 pp.10-11
- The New Cambridge English Course 4 pp.41,74-75
- Think First Certificate [Revised] pp.96-99
- Workout Upper Intermediate pp.79-80,82

Advanced
- Advanced Communication Games No.4
- Advanced Vocabulary and Idiom pp.19,82-83
- Distinction pp.104-107
- English Vocabulary In Use pp.66-69,156-157
- Headway Advanced pp.62-63
- Language Issues pp.13-14
- Progress To Proficiency (New Edition) pp.48-49
- Test Your Vocabulary 4 p.8
- Wordbuilder pp.25-35,39-41
- Workout Advanced pp.51-52

DESCRIBING PEOPLE contd.

Various
- Keep Talking Activity No.11
- More Grammar Games p.97
- Writing Games Activity No.12

DESCRIBING PICTURES

Upper Intermediate
- Think First Certificate [Revised] pp.136-137

DESCRIBING PLACES

Beginner/Elementary
- Blueprint One pp.27-28
- Look Ahead 1 pp.40-41 [rooms]
- Headway Elementary pp.69-75

Pre-Intermediate
- Language In Use Pre-Intermediate pp.65-67

Early/Mid-Intermediate
- Headway Intermediate pp.30-32,36,52-53
- Look Ahead Intermediate pp.20-21,24
- New Headway Intermediate pp.63-64 [rooms]
- Think Ahead to First Certificate p.132 [rooms]

Upper Intermediate
- First Certificate Gold pp.136-138
- Headway Upper Intermediate pp.72-73 [Cardiff]

Advanced
- Advanced Communication Games No.8
- Headway Advanced p.61 [rooms]
- Wordbuilder pp.78-79

GIVING DIRECTIONS

Beginner/Elementary
- Conversation Pieces pp.9-12
- Elementary Communication Games No.19
- Elementary Task Listening pp.42-43
- Headway Elementary pp.39, 75
- Look Ahead 1 pp.102-107
- Play Games With English 1 pp.82-83
- The Beginners' Choice pp.97-98

- The New Cambridge English Course 1 pp.26-27
- True To Life Elementary pp.103-104

Pre-Intermediate
- Blueprint Two pp.19-20
- Headway Pre-Intermediate p.47
- Language In Use Pre-Intermediate p.65
- Pre-Intermediate Matters p.78
- Reward Pre-Intermediate pp.32-33
- Streamline Connections Unit 50
- The New Cambridge English Course 2 p.113
- True To Life Pre-Intermediate pp.19-20

Early/Mid-Intermediate
- Everyday Listening and Speaking - Making Headway pp.30-32
- Meanings Into Words Intermediate pp.25-26
- Task Listening pp.20-21
- Think Ahead to First Certificate p.75

Advanced
- Wordbuilder pp.21-24

OFFERING, ACCEPTING AND REFUSING HELP

Early/Mid-Intermediate
- Headway Intermediate pp.18-19
- Workout Intermediate p.97

Upper Intermediate
- English Grammar Lessons pp.12-15

MAKING INVITATIONS

Beginner/Elementary
- Elementary Communication Games Nos.26-27
- True To Life Elementary pp.144-145

Pre-Intermediate
- Headway Pre-Intermediate p.64
- Reward Pre-Intermediate pp.38-39

Early/Mid-Intermediate
- English Grammar In Use pp.72-73

EXPRESSING LIKES/DISLIKES/PREFERENCES

Beginner/Elementary
- Blueprint One pp.25-26
- Conversation Pieces pp.17-20
- Elementary Communication Games No.22
- Headstart pp.32-35
- Play Games With English 1 pp.36-37
- The New Cambridge English Course 1 p.28
- True To Life Elementary pp.50-54

Pre-Intermediate
- Reward Pre-Intermediate pp.8-9

Early/Mid-Intermediate
- Intermediate Communication Games No.35

Upper Intermediate
- Blueprint Upper Intermediate p.15

Advanced
- Advanced Communication Games No.34
- English Vocabulary In Use pp.138-139

Various
- Keep Talking Activity No.79
- More Grammar Games p.61

MAKING OFFERS

Beginner/Elementary
- True To Life Elementary pp.145-146

Pre-Intermediate
- The New Cambridge English Course 2 pp.108-109
- True To Life Pre-Intermediate p.123-125

Early/Mid-Intermediate
- English Grammar In Use pp.72-73
- New Headway Intermediate p.44
- Language In Use Intermediate p.110
- Meanings Into Words Intermediate pp.47-49

Advanced
- Advanced Communication Games No.17

EXPRESSING OPINIONS

Beginner/Elementary
- Elementary Communication Games No.35
- The New Cambridge English Course 1 p.94

Pre-Intermediate
- Pre-Intermediate Matters pp.56-57

Early/Mid-Intermediate
- Intermediate Communication Games No.17
- Look Ahead Intermediate p.85
- New Headway Intermediate p.34

Upper Intermediate
- First Certificate Gold p.62
- Look Ahead Upper Intermediate pp.12-13
- Meanings Into Words Upper Intermediate pp.31-38
- Think First Certificate [Revised] p.90

Advanced
- Advanced Communication Games No.30
- Distinction pp.52,73
- English Vocabulary In Use pp.134-135

ASKING/GIVING PERMISSION

Beginner/Elementary
- Elementary Communication Games No.32
- The New Cambridge English Course 1 p.92

Pre-Intermediate
- Language In Use Pre-Intermediate p.77
- Reward Pre-Intermediate pp.66-67,70-71
- Workout Pre-Intermediate p.47

Early/Mid-Intermediate
- English Grammar In Use pp.72-73
- Headway Intermediate pp.55-56
- Language In Use Intermediate p.26
- Meanings Into Words Intermediate p.46

Upper Intermediate
- English Grammar Lessons pp.48-51
- Workout Upper Intermediate p.89

PERSUADING

Advanced
- Workout Advanced p.44

Section 3: Topics

The Index: *Topics*

ACCOMMODATION (SEE HOUSING)

ADVENTURE

Beginner/Elementary
- Headway Elementary pp.86-87
- True To Life Elementary pp.88-89

Pre-Intermediate
- Headway Pre-Intermediate pp.84-85 [confrontation with a tiger]

Early/Mid-Intermediate
- Intermediate Matters p.24 [adventure walking holiday]

Upper Intermediate
- Blueprint Upper Intermediate pp.8-11
- First Certificate Gold pp.6-11
- New First Certificate Masterclass pp.72-73
- Upper Intermediate Matters pp.62 [journey to the jungle],143 [journey into the interior]
- Workout Upper Intermediate pp.24,74

Advanced
- Progress To Proficiency (New Edition) pp.19-35
- The Nelson Proficiency Course pp.140-142 [lost at sea]

ADVERTISING

Pre-Intermediate
- Blueprint Two pp.42-43
- Headway Pre-Intermediate p.31

Early/Mid-Intermediate
- Intermediate Vocabulary p.34
- Listening Intermediate [Oxford Supp. Skills] pp.13-17
- Meanings Into Words Intermediate pp.64-65
- The Intermediate Choice p.88

Upper Intermediate
- Workout Upper Intermediate pp.98-100,102

Advanced
- Advanced Vocabulary and Idiom p.3
- Distinction pp.136-140
- Focus On Proficiency pp.173-178
- Proficiency Masterclass p.155
- Progress To Proficiency (New Edition) pp.103-105,109-110

- Speaking Personally pp.18-19
- The Nelson Proficiency Course pp.173-174

Various
- Keep Talking Activity No.58
- The Q Book pp.78-79,111-114
- Writing Games Activity No.22

ANIMALS

Beginner/Elementary
- Play Games With English 1 pp.34-35
- Listening Elementary [Oxford Supp. Skills] pp.38-39
- Start Testing Your Vocabulary pp.68-69

Pre-Intermediate
- Blueprint Two pp.45-46, [dolphins],109-110 [elephants]
- Headway Pre-Intermediate p.9
- Language In Use Pre-Intermediate p.35 [Aesop's fables]
- Look Ahead 2 pp.66-67
- Streamline Connections Unit 27
- Workout Pre-Intermediate pp.31-33

Early/Mid-Intermediate
- A Way With Words 2 pp.46-49
- Intermediate Matters pp.111-116,140-141
- Intermediate Vocabulary p.39 [animal sounds],47 [young animals]
- Listening Intermediate [Oxford Supp. Skills] pp.34-40 [lost dog]
- Look Ahead Intermediate pp.84-85 [circuses]
- Reading Intermediate [Oxford Supp. Skills] pp.1-4,21-28
- Speaking Intermediate [Oxford Supp. Skills] pp.26-27
- Test Your Vocabulary 2 p.25 [animal sounds]
- The Intermediate Choice pp.102,103
- Vocabulary Builder 1 pp.60-61

Upper Intermediate
- English Vocabulary In Use pp.146-47
- First Certificate Gold pp.134,135
- Headway Upper Intermediate pp.86-87
- Look Ahead Upper Intermediate pp.26-27 [guide dogs]
- Meanings Into Words Upper Intermediate pp.48-49
- Test Your Vocabulary 3 p.33 [insects]
- The New Cambridge English Course 4 pp.88-89
- Think First Certificate [Revised] pp.41 [living with snakes],116-125

ANIMALS contd.

- Upper Intermediate Matters p.126 [animal experimentation]

Advanced
- Advanced Vocabulary and Idiom pp.54-55
- Distinction pp.75-80
- English Vocabulary In Use pp.146-47
- Focus On Proficiency pp.189-190
- Language Issues pp.92-99
- Proficiency Masterclass pp.116-128
- Progress To Proficiency (New Edition) pp.147-148 [save the whales]
- Reading Advanced [Oxford Supp. Skills] pp.43-59 [animal language]
- Test Your Vocabulary 4 p.1
- The Nelson Proficiency Course pp.59-76
- Wordbuilder pp.82-86
- Workout Advanced pp.64,65

Various
- Discussions That Work pp.81-83 [zoo plan]
- Grammar Games pp.100 101
- Grammar Practice Activities p.256
- The Anti-Grammar Grammar Book pp.12-13,83
- Writing Games Activity No.3

ART

Pre-Intermediate
- Blueprint Two pp.59-60 [Van Gogh]
- Language In Use Pre-Intermediate pp.106-109
- Workout Pre-Intermediate pp.58-59 [graffiti],70 [murals]

Early/Mid-Intermediate
- Intermediate Vocabulary p.34
- Listening Intermediate [Oxford Supp. Skills] pp.22-25
- Look Ahead Intermediate pp.104-105
- New Headway Intermediate pp.29-32
- Think Ahead to First Certificate pp.54-56
- True To Life Intermediate pp.137-140

Upper Intermediate
- Look Ahead Upper Intermediate pp.80-81
- New First Certificate Masterclass pp.42-43
- The New Cambridge English Course 4 pp.104-105

Advanced
- Headway Advanced pp.63-65
- Language Issues pp.52-53
- Proficiency Masterclass pp.72-81
- Progress To Proficiency (New Edition) pp.229-231
- Wordbuilder pp.171-172
- Workout Advanced pp.109-115

Various
- Writing Games Activity Nos.29-30

BODY

Beginner/Elementary
- Start Testing Your Vocabulary pp.3 [the face],7
- The Beginners' Choice pp.54-57,62

Pre-Intermediate
- Look Ahead 2 pp.80-87
- Reward Pre-Intermediate p.50
- Test Your Vocabulary 1 p.22
- The Pre-Intermediate Choice p.15
- True To Life Pre-Intermediate pp.30-33

Early/Mid-Intermediate
- Intermediate Vocabulary pp.41-42 [body movements],52
- Vocabulary Builder 1 pp.8-29

Upper Intermediate
- English Vocabulary In Use pp.144-145
- First Certificate Gold p.84
- Headway Upper Intermediate pp.3-4
- New First Certificate Masterclass p.87
- Test Your Vocabulary 3 pp.26,31,75-76

Advanced
- Advanced Vocabulary and Idiom pp.7,55
- Distinction pp.105/106
- English Vocabulary In Use pp.144-145
- Focus On Advanced English pp.185-200
- Test Your Vocabulary 4 p.9
- The Nelson Proficiency Course p.188
- Wordbuilder pp.25-35

Various
- More Grammar Games pp.40-41

BOOKS

Early/Mid-Intermediate
- Intermediate Vocabulary p.7 [books and reading]
- Test Your Vocabulary 2 pp.56-57
- Vocabulary Builder 2 pp.50-51 [reading]

Upper Intermediate
- Think First Certificate [Revised] pp.28-29

Advanced
- Advanced Vocabulary and Idiom pp.7-8
- Listening Advanced [Oxford Supp. Skills] pp.12-19
- Distinction pp.118-120
- Progress To Proficiency (New Edition) pp.162-175
- Workout Advanced pp.86-91

BRITAIN AND THE USA

Beginner/Elementary
- Conversation Pieces pp.37-40
- Play Games With English 1 pp.72-73

Pre-Intermediate
- Reward Pre-Intermediate pp.8-9,56-57
- The New Cambridge English Course 2 pp.52-53
- Workout Pre-Intermediate p.101

Early/Mid-Intermediate
- Headway Intermediate p.36
- Intermediate Matters p.26
- New Blueprint Intermediate pp.58-59,68-69

Upper Intermediate
- Think First Certificate [Revised] pp.160-173

Advanced
- Headway Advanced pp.35-37

BUSINESS

Beginner/Elementary
- Elementary Task Listening pp.14-15 [arranging a business meeting]

Pre-Intermediate
- The Pre-Intermediate Choice pp.26-28

Early/Mid-Intermediate
- Headway Intermediate pp.39-40
- Help With Phrasal Verbs pp.5-8 [arranging a meeting], 16-20 [company success and failure],59-62 [borrowing money to open a restaurant]
- Look Ahead Intermediate pp.44-45

Upper Intermediate
- Look Ahead Upper Intermediate p.39 [opening a restaurant]
- Test Your Vocabulary 3 pp.50-51

Advanced
- Progress To Proficiency (New Edition) pp.203-207
- Wordbuilder pp.181-184

Various
- Discussions That Work pp.116-117

CARS AND MOTORING

Beginner/Elementary
- Elementary Task Listening pp.26-27

Pre-Intermediate
- Everyday Listening and Speaking - Making Headway pp.40-42 [hiring a car]
- Headway Pre-Intermediate pp.69, 82-83 [Volkswagen Beetle]
- Language In Use Pre-Intermediate pp.100-101
- Look Ahead 2 pp.38-43
- Streamline Connections Unit 58
- Test Your Vocabulary 1 p.21
- Workout Pre-Intermediate p.50

Early/Mid-Intermediate
- Headway Intermediate p.59
- Intermediate Vocabulary p.8
- Language In Use Intermediate p.55
- Look Ahead Intermediate p.42
- Task Listening pp.24-25 [hiring a car],36-37 [phoning a garage], 48 [parking in London]
- Test Your Vocabulary 2 p.40
- The New Cambridge English Course 3 pp.86-87
- Vocabulary Builder 1 pp.70-71
- Workout Intermediate p.60

CARS AND MOTORING contd.

Upper Intermediate
- Phrasal Verbs and Idioms [Making Headway] pp.59-63
- Test Your Vocabulary 3 pp.44-45
- The New Cambridge English Course 4 pp.20-21
- Think First Certificate [Revised] (pp.86-87
- Upper Intermediate Matters pp.47-49,51

Advanced
- Advanced Vocabulary and Idiom p.12
- Distinction p.28
- Wordbuilder pp.101-10

Various
- The Q Book pp.20-23 [motor accident],83 [the driving instructor],126

CELEBRATIONS

Beginner/Elementary
- Headway Elementary pp.52-53 [special occasions]
- The Beginners' Choice p.92
- True To Life Elementary pp.142-145

Pre-Intermediate
- Look Ahead 2 pp.102-107
- Pre-Intermediate Matters pp.102-106
- Reward Pre-Intermediate pp.54-55

Early/Mid-Intermediate
- Meanings Into Words Intermediate pp.73-74 [Hallowe'en],169-170 [carnival]

Upper Intermediate
- Look Ahead Upper Intermediate pp.100-101 [festivals]
- New First Certificate Masterclass pp.164-165,167
- Think First Certificate [Revised] pp.128-129

CHARITY

Early/Mid-Intermediate
- Headway Intermediate pp.61-63
- New Headway Intermediate p.83

Upper Intermediate
- The New Cambridge English Course 4 pp.64-65
- Look Ahead Upper Intermediate pp.92-93

Advanced
- Proficiency Masterclass pp.96-97
- Speaking Advanced [Oxford Supp. Skills] pp.51-53

CHILDREN/CHILDHOOD

Beginner/Elementary
- The New Cambridge English Course 1 p.53

Pre-Intermediate
- The Pre-Intermediate Choice pp.90-91 [punishing children]

Early/Mid-Intermediate
- Look Ahead Intermediate pp.108-109
- Intermediate Vocabulary p.33

Upper Intermediate
- Headway Upper Intermediate p.62 [childhood in the 3rd World]
- Look Ahead Upper Intermediate p.124
- Upper Intermediate Matters p.4,7,10-13 [ways of bringing up children]

Advanced
- Advanced Vocabulary and Idiom p.3
- Distinction pp.112-117 [children's language]
- Headway Advanced pp.43-48 [bringing up children]
- Speaking Personally pp.72-73

Various
- The Q Book p.90

CINEMA/THEATRE

Beginner/Elementary
- Reading Elementary [Oxford Supp. Skills] pp.32-33 [Shakespeare]

Pre-Intermediate
- True To Life Pre-Intermediate pp.153-156

Early/Mid-Intermediate
- Intermediate Matters p.8 [interview with Judi Dench]
- Intermediate Vocabulary pp.9,26
- Look Ahead Intermediate pp.82-83
- New Blueprint Intermediate p.65 [Shakespeare]
- Task Listening pp.42-43
- The Intermediate Choice pp.74-76
- True To Life Intermediate pp.50-52 [actors]

CINEMA/THEATRE contd.

- New First Certificate Masterclass pp.112-118
- Think First Certificate [Revised] pp.36/37 [dangers of London],138-147
- Upper Intermediate Matters pp.84-89

Advanced
- Advanced Vocabulary and Idiom p.5
- Distinction pp.15-22
- English Vocabulary In Use pp.110-111
- Focus On Proficiency pp.95-113
- Headway Advanced pp.74-78
- Language Issues p.107
- Phrasal Verbs and Idioms [Making Headway] pp.40-45
- Proficiency Masterclass pp.141-142,162-163,165-168
- Test Your Vocabulary 4 pp.34-35
- The Nelson Proficiency Course pp.101-106,146-148 [solitary confinement]
- Wordbuilder pp.185-187

Various
- Discussions That Work pp.58-60 [alibi],63 [picture story],77-78 ['prisoners']
- Grammar Games pp.106-107
- The Q Book pp.101-103

CULTURAL DIFFERENCES

Beginner/Elementary
- Look Ahead 1 pp.98-99 [eating out/eating habits]
- The Beginners' Choice p.30 [politeness], p.62 [body language], p.92 [celebrations], p.124 [education]

Pre-Intermediate
- Headway Pre-Intermediate pp.13,16
- Look Ahead 2 p.85 [body language]
- The Pre-Intermediate Choice pp.30 [lifestyles],60 [money],90 [attitudes to children],120 [marriage]
- Pre-Intermediate Matters pp.60-61 [Britain and the British],114
- Reward Pre-Intermediate pp.2-3
- Workout Pre-Intermediate p.100 [personal space]

Early/Mid-Intermediate
- New Blueprint Intermediate pp.74-75
- Headway Intermediate pp.20-22 [cultural stereotyping]
- New Headway Intermediate pp.39-41
- Intermediate Matters pp.26-27

- The Intermediate Choice pp.32 [social issues],64 [health and exercise],90 [good manners],120 [the press]
- Language In Use Intermediate pp.30-31
- Meanings Into Words Intermediate p.125
- Think Ahead to First Certificate p.73,82-83 [typical Englishman],90-93 [body language etc.]

Upper Intermediate
- Look Ahead Upper Intermediate pp.96-99
- Upper Intermediate Matters pp.98-103

Advanced
- Focus On Advanced English pp.179-180,191-192
- Headway Advanced pp.37-39
- Language Issues pp.136-137
- Workout Advanced pp.42-43

CUSTOMS/CEREMONIES

Pre-Intermediate
- Language In Use Pre-Intermediate p.18

Early/Mid-Intermediate
- Language In Use Intermediate p.90

Upper Intermediate
- A Way With Words 3 pp.81-85
- Upper Intermediate Matters pp.128,132,134

DISASTERS

Pre-Intermediate
- Streamline Connections Unit 23

Early/Mid-Intermediate
- Intermediate Vocabulary p.20

Upper Intermediate
- First Certificate Gold p.117

DREAMS

Beginner/Elementary
- Speaking Elementary [Oxford Supp. Skills] pp.40-47

DREAMS contd.

ECCENTRICS

EDUCATION

EMBARRASSING EXPERIENCES

FILMS

Pre-Intermediate
- Headway Pre-Intermediate pp.52-53 [Paul Newman]
- The Pre-Intermediate Choice pp.44,46-47
- Workout Pre-Intermediate p.12

Early/Mid-Intermediate
- Intermediate Vocabulary p.9
- Look Ahead Intermediate pp.18-19 [visit to a film studio]
- New Blueprint Intermediate pp.24-25 [Antonio Banderas]
- Think Ahead to First Certificate pp.16-23

Upper Intermediate
- Blueprint Upper Intermediate pp.38-39
- Meanings Into Words Upper Intermediate pp.40-41
- New First Certificate Masterclass pp.178-179
- Upper Intermediate Matters p.75

Advanced
- Distinction pp.81-88
- Language Issues pp.67-75
- Progress To Proficiency (New Edition) pp.219-223

Various
- Writing Games Activity No.32

FOOD/COOKING

Beginner/Elementary
- Blueprint One pp.53-54
- Conversation Pieces pp.25-28
- Elementary Communication Games Nos.8-10
- Elementary Task Listening p.18 [deciding where to eat]
- Headstart pp.22,60-61
- Headway Elementary pp.66-67
- Look Ahead 1 pp.30-35,96-101
- Reading Elementary [Oxford Supp. Skills] pp.22-23
- Speaking Elementary [Oxford Supp. Skills] pp.28-29
- Start Testing Your Vocabulary pp.22-23,29,32
- The Beginners' Choice pp.6-8, 72-74
- True To Life Elementary pp.19-23

Pre-Intermediate
- A Way With Words 1 pp.18-22
- Everyday Listening and Speaking - Making Headway pp.37-39 [friends for dinner]
- Headway Pre-Intermediate pp.30-31
- Language In Use Pre-Intermediate pp.28-31
- Look Ahead 2 pp.58-63
- Pre-Intermediate Matters pp.36-40
- Reward Pre-Intermediate pp.34-35
- Test Your Vocabulary 1 pp.20,38-39
- The Pre-Intermediate Choice pp.96 [products/packages],97 [chocolate]
- True To Life Pre-Intermediate pp.57-61
- Workout Pre-Intermediate pp.64-67

Early/Mid-Intermediate
- Headway Intermediate pp.26-27 [English food]
- Intermediate Matters pp.81,104-109
- Intermediate Vocabulary p.14
- New Headway Intermediate pp.60-61
- Speaking Intermediate [Oxford Supp. Skills] pp.40-46
- The Intermediate Choice pp.79-80,82
- Think Ahead to First Certificate pp.46-47 [problems of being overweight], 86-91
- Vocabulary Builder 2 pp.20-25
- Workout Intermediate pp.68-70

Upper Intermediate
- A Way With Words 3 pp.84-85
- Blueprint Upper Intermediate p.53
- First Certificate Gold pp.88-91
- Headway Upper Intermediate pp.47-48
- Meanings Into Words Upper Intermediate pp.120-121 [dieting]
- Test Your Vocabulary 3 pp.42-43
- Workout Upper Intermediate pp.92,94 [vegetarianism etc.]

Advanced
- Advanced Vocabulary and Idiom pp.12-13,60
- Distinction pp.68-74
- English Vocabulary In Use pp.86-87
- Focus On Proficiency pp.179-181
- Progress To Proficiency (New Edition) pp.65-78
- Speaking Personally pp.20-27
- Wordbuilder pp.87-90,173-177
- Writing Advanced [Oxford Supp. Skills] pp.103-113

Various
- Discussions That Work p.64 [picture sequence]

HEALTH AND HEALTH CARE

Beginner/Elementary
- Blueprint One pp.105-106

HOBBIES

HOLIDAYS/HOTELS

Beginner/Elementary
- Elementary Communication Games No.16 [reserving hotel accommodation],38 [holiday quiz]
- Elementary Task Listening pp.12-13,20-21 [talking about holiday photographs],36-37 [visiting the sights]
- Elementary Vocabulary pp.18-19
- Listening Elementary [Oxford Supp. Skills] pp.14-19
- Look Ahead 1 pp.80-85
- Speaking Elementary [Oxford Supp. Skills] pp.26-27
- The Beginners' Choice pp.40-44

Pre-Intermediate
- A Way With Words 1 pp.37-41
- Blueprint Two pp.23-24
- Everyday Listening and Speaking - Making Headway pp.25-27 [hotels],28-30 [going sightseeing]
- Headway Pre-Intermediate pp.63-64
- Language In Use Pre-Intermediate p.52
- Pre-Intermediate Matters pp.120-122
- Test Your Vocabulary 1 p.41
- The New Cambridge English Course 2 pp.52-53
- The Pre-Intermediate Choice p.18
- Workout Pre-Intermediate pp.90-91

Early/Mid-Intermediate
- Task Listening pp.8-9 [sightseeing]
- Everyday Listening and Speaking - Making Headway pp.33-36 [booking in to a hotel]
- Headway Intermediate p.17 [a disastrous holiday]
- New Headway Intermediate pp.32-33,51-53
- Intermediate Matters pp.76-79 [hotels]
- The Intermediate Choice pp.45-46
- Language In Use Intermediate pp.28-29
- Look Ahead Intermediate pp.28-29 [postcards],56-61,120-125
- True To Life Intermediate pp.82 [igloo hotel],117-118
- Meanings Into Words Intermediate p.124
- Workout Intermediate p.26

Upper Intermediate
- Phrasal Verbs and Idioms [Making Headway] pp.33-37
- English Vocabulary In Use pp.100-101
- Blueprint Upper Intermediate pp.70-71
- Think First Certificate [Revised] pp.60-67

Advanced
- Focus On Advanced English pp.80-90

Various
- Keep Talking Activity Nos.100,109
- Grammar Practice Activities pp.113-117

HOROSCOPES/ZODIAC

Beginner/Elementary
- The New Cambridge English Course 1 p.114

Upper Intermediate
- Meanings Into Words Upper Intermediate pp.37-38,136
- Test Your Vocabulary 3 p.20

Advanced
- Language Issues pp.13-14

Various
- Grammar Practice Activities pp.118-119

HOUSING

Beginner/Elementary
- Blueprint One pp.41-42
- Elementary Communication Games No.11
- Look Ahead 1 pp.36-43
- Start Testing Your Vocabulary pp.37,40
- The Beginners' Choice pp.116-117
- The New Cambridge English Course 1 pp.24,39

Pre-Intermediate
- A Way With Words 1 pp.6-11
- Blueprint Two p.37 [homeless]
- Language In Use Pre-Intermediate pp.38-41
- Pre-Intermediate Matters pp.54-55,58 [rooms],109 [neighbours]
- Reward Pre-Intermediate pp.6-7
- True To Life Pre-Intermediate pp.92-93,111-112 [rooms]

Early/Mid-Intermediate
- A Way With Words 2 pp.10-13
- Everyday Listening and Speaking - Making Headway pp.37-40 [looking for somewhere to live]
- Intermediate Communication Games No.11
- Intermediate Vocabulary pp.13,43
- Language In Use Intermediate pp.12-15
- Look Ahead Intermediate pp.10-13

HOUSING contd.

- Task Listening pp.10-11 [finding out the house rules], 12-13 [phoning a flat-owner],38 [flat hunting]
- Test Your Vocabulary 2 p.12 [rooms]
- The Intermediate Choice pp.36-39 [neighbours]
- True To Life Intermediate pp.102-103 [neighbours]
- Vocabulary Builder 2 pp.8-11

Upper Intermediate
- English Vocabulary In Use pp.72-73
- Meanings Into Words Upper Intermediate pp.83-84
- Phrasal Verbs and Idioms [Making Headway] pp.19-23
- The New Cambridge English Course 4 pp.66-67

Advanced
- English Vocabulary In Use pp.72-73
- Focus On Proficiency pp.4-18,60-61 [neighbours]
- Speaking Advanced [Oxford Supp. Skills] pp.77-79
- The Nelson Proficiency Course p.13
- Wordbuilder pp.94-95

HUMOUR

Early/Mid-Intermediate
- Vocabulary Builder 2 pp.40-41
- Speaking Intermediate [Oxford Supp. Skills] pp.21-25
- Intermediate Matters p.5 [Lenny Henry]
- Language In Use Intermediate pp.100-101 [smiling, laughing]

Advanced
- Speaking Personally pp.86-98
- Test Your Vocabulary 5 pp.22-23
- Distinction pp.130-131
- The Nelson Proficiency Course pp.143-145 [puns]
- Workout Advanced pp.6-7

INTELLIGENCE

Beginner/Elementary
- Headway Elementary p.43
Early/Mid-Intermediate
- Headway Intermediate pp.56-57 [child prodigy]
- Vocabulary Builder 1 pp.44-45

Upper Intermediate
- First Certificate Gold pp.58-59

Advanced
- Headway Advanced pp.116-120 [the brain etc.]
- Speaking Personally pp.40-47

INVENTIONS

Beginner/Elementary
- Look Ahead 1 pp.76-77 [inventor's daily routine]

Pre-Intermediate
- Look Ahead 2 pp.44-45

Early/Mid-Intermediate
- Language In Use Intermediate pp.36,48-49

Upper Intermediate
- First Certificate Gold pp.105-106

JOBS (SEE WORK)

KIDNAP

Early/Mid-Intermediate
- Intermediate Matters p.19
- Think Ahead to First Certificate p.33

LANGUAGE/LEARNING LANGUAGES

Beginner/Elementary
- Writing Elementary [Oxford Supp. Skills] pp.46-51

The Index: *Topics*

LANGUAGE/LEARNING LANGUAGES contd.

Pre-Intermediate
- Everyday Listening and Speaking - Making Headway pp.53-55 [choosing an English course]
- Look Ahead 2 pp.16-17
- Reward Pre-Intermediate pp.56-57 [British v. American English]
- The Pre-Intermediate Choice p.63
- True To Life Pre-Intermediate pp.36-41

Early/Mid-Intermediate
- Help With Phrasal Verbs pp.1-4
- Meanings Into Words Intermediate p.126
- Task Listening p.22 [enquiring about a language course]
- The New Cambridge English Course 3 pp.14-15
- Workout Intermediate pp.8-11

Upper Intermediate
- First Certificate Gold pp.150-158
- Headway Upper Intermediate pp.1-5
- Speaking Upper Intermediate [Oxford Supp. Skills] pp.57-58
- The New Cambridge English Course 4 pp.30-31
- Think First Certificate [Revised] pp.10-11,16-17
- Workout Upper Intermediate p.12

Advanced
- Distinction pp.39-44,148-153
- Focus On Advanced English pp.55-66
- Headway Advanced pp.6-7,66-69 [Pygmalion]
- Language Issues pp.6,29-30
- Proficiency Masterclass pp.102-113
- Progress To Proficiency (New Edition) pp.51-53
- The Nelson Proficiency Course pp.203-221

Various
- The Q Book p.131

LEISURE

Beginner/Elementary
- Conversation Pieces pp.21-24
- Headway Elementary pp.28-29
- Listening Elementary [Oxford Supp. Skills] pp.26-30
- Look Ahead 1 pp.66-71
- Start Testing Your Vocabulary pp.54-57

Pre-Intermediate
- Blueprint Two pp.9-10

- Language In Use Pre-Intermediate pp.72-75
- Look Ahead 2 pp.8-15
- Pre-Intermediate Matters pp.67,70,88
- Workout Pre-Intermediate pp.6-9

Early/Mid-Intermediate
- Everyday Listening and Speaking - Making Headway pp.11-14
- Headway Intermediate p.3
- Intermediate Matters pp.4,96-102
- Intermediate Vocabulary p.7 (books & reading)
- Meanings Into Words Intermediate pp.91-97
- True To Life Intermediate p.20
- Vocabulary Builder 2 pp.36-39,50-53

Upper Intermediate
- Meanings Into Words Upper Intermediate pp.3,68-69 [party-goer quiz]
- The New Cambridge English Course 4 pp.8-9
- Think First Certificate [Revised] pp.22-23

Advanced
- Advanced Vocabulary and Idiom pp.7-8 [books],10-11 [drinking]
- Distinction pp.8-14 [sport and games]
- Proficiency Masterclass pp.173-183
- Progress To Proficiency (New Edition) pp.3-18

LITERATURE

Beginner/Elementary
- Headway Elementary p.51 [Charles Dickens], pp.95-97

Pre-Intermediate
- Headway Pre-Intermediate pp.24-25 [interview with Ian Fleming]

Early/Mid-Intermediate
- Intermediate Vocabulary p.7 [books & reading]
- New Blueprint Intermediate pp.30-31 [extract from Cider With Rosie]
- New Headway Intermediate pp.29-32,121-122 [David Copperfield]

Upper Intermediate
- Blueprint Upper Intermediate pp.60-62,74-76
- Headway Upper Intermediate pp.93-94 [Jack Higgins]
- Look Ahead Upper Intermediate pp.68-69 [extracts from Silas Marner]
- Upper Intermediate Matters pp.69-74 [extracts from Kazuo Ishiguro story]

LITERATURE

Advanced
- Advanced Vocabulary and Idiom pp.7-8 [books]
- Distinction pp.118-124
- Headway Advanced pp.23-30,84-91
- Language Issues pp.67-70,124 [interview with P.D.James]
- Proficiency Masterclass pp.22-23,104-105 [Dickens]
- Progress To Proficiency (New Edition) pp.162-175
- The Listening File pp.60-63 [interview with a poet]
- The Nelson Proficiency Course pp.114-115 [extract from Jane Eyre]

LOVE AND RELATIONSHIPS

Beginner/Elementary
- Headway Elementary p.59
- Reading Elementary [Oxford Supp. Skills] pp.2-11
- The Beginners' Choice pp.66-69

Pre-Intermediate
- Headway Pre-Intermediate pp.38-39,117 [song]
- Language In Use Pre-Intermediate pp.14-15 [are you a loner?]
- Look Ahead 2 pp.106-107 [weddings]
- Pre-Intermediate Matters pp.79,82
- The Pre-Intermediate Choice pp.120-121
- True To Life Pre-Intermediate pp.76-81

Early/Mid-Intermediate
- Headway Intermediate p.84 [marriage and divorce]
- Help With Phrasal Verbs pp. 13-15
- Intermediate Matters pp.51-52
- Intermediate Vocabulary p.22
- New Headway Intermediate pp.86-87,116-120
- Speaking Intermediate [Oxford Supp. Skills] pp.53-61
- The Intermediate Choice pp.8-9 (Japanese Royal Wedding)
- The New Cambridge English Course 3 pp.62-63
- Think Ahead to First Certificate pp.120-123 [Royal romance]
- True To Life Intermediate pp.37-38,63-65 [weddings]
- Vocabulary Builder 1 pp.38-41
- Workout Intermediate pp.44-45 [Lonely Hearts ads.]

Upper Intermediate
- English Vocabulary In Use pp.70-71
- First Certificate Gold pp.46-54
- Headway Upper Intermediate pp.79-80 [arranged marriage]
- Meanings Into Words Upper Intermediate pp.24-25
- Phrasal Verbs and Idioms [Making Headway] pp.70-75
- The New Cambridge English Course 4 pp.86-87
- Upper Intermediate Matters pp.91-96 [marriage]
- Workout Upper Intermediate pp.63-65,68, p.66 [friendship], pp.69-72 [marriage]

Advanced
- Advanced Vocabulary and Idiom pp.4,14 [friends]
- English Vocabulary In Use pp.70-71
- Focus On Proficiency pp.55-72
- Phrasal Verbs and Idioms [Making Headway] pp.58-63
- Proficiency Masterclass pp.139-140
- Progress To Proficiency (New Edition) pp.191-202
- Speaking Personally pp.68-69
- Wordbuilder pp.135-136

Various
- Discussions That Work pp.61 [picture sequence],84-86 ['couples']
- Writing Games Activity Nos.26,38

MEDIA

Pre-Intermediate
- Pre-Intermediate Matters pp.97,100 [newspaper stories]

Early/Mid-Intermediate
- Headway Intermediate pp.81-83 [newspapers]
- Help With Phrasal Verbs pp.39-42
- Intermediate Vocabulary p.25
- Language In Use Intermediate pp.64-67
- Look Ahead Intermediate pp.96-101 [newspapers]
- The Intermediate Choice pp.120-121 [the press]
- Think Ahead to First Certificate pp.102-109 [newspapers]

MONEY contd.

Advanced
- Advanced Vocabulary and Idiom pp.17-18
- English Vocabulary In Use pp.112-113
- Phrasal Verbs and Idioms [Making Headway] pp.35-39
- The Nelson Proficiency Course pp.31-33 [gambling],40-55
- Wordbuilder pp.146-148
- Workout Advanced pp.61,68

Various
- Keep Talking Activity No.81
- The Q Book pp.127-129 [spending patterns]

MUSIC

Pre-Intermediate
- Blueprint Two pp.13-14
- Headway Pre-Intermediate pp.54-55 [interview with a musician]
- Streamline Connections Unit 68 [Elvis Presley biography]
- The Pre-Intermediate Choice pp.57-58,111-112
- Workout Pre-Intermediate pp.40-43

Early/Mid-Intermediate
- Intermediate Vocabulary p.19
- New Headway Intermediate pp.29-32
- Think Ahead to First Certificate pp.29 [riot at a pop concert],59 [biography of Mozart]
- Vocabulary Builder 2 pp.46-47

Upper Intermediate
- New First Certificate Masterclass pp.190-191
- Test Your Vocabulary 3 p.70
- Upper Intermediate Matters p.5 [interview with Gloria Estefan]
- Workout Upper Intermediate p.10

Advanced
- Progress To Proficiency (New Edition) pp.5-7,226-227
- The Listening File pp.24-27,32-35
- Wordbuilder pp.168-170

NEIGHBOURS (SEE HOUSING)

NUMBERS

Beginner/Elementary
- Elementary Vocabulary p.55
- Headway Elementary p.59
- Look Ahead 1 p.24
- Play Games With English 2 pp.16-17
- The Beginners' Choice pp.9,33
- The New Cambridge English Course 1 pp.12-13

Pre-Intermediate
- Headway Pre-Intermediate p.18
- Reward Pre-Intermediate p.46
- The Pre-Intermediate Choice p.116

Early/Mid-Intermediate
- New Headway Intermediate p.23
- The Intermediate Choice pp.9, 34-5

Upper Intermediate
- First Certificate Gold p.103
- Headway Upper Intermediate p.9
- Think First Certificate [Revised] p.163

Advanced
- Advanced Vocabulary and Idiom p.18
- Distinction p.25
- Test Your Vocabulary 4 p.22

Various
- Grammar Practice Activities pp.191-196

OLD AGE

Beginner/Elementary
- Headway Elementary pp.102-103
- True To Life Elementary p.120

Pre-Intermediate
- Headway Pre-Intermediate p.76
- Look Ahead 2 p.92

Early/Mid-Intermediate
- Headway Intermediate pp.34-35,40-41 (retired managing director), pp.50-51 [longevity quiz]
- New Headway Intermediate pp.73-74 [retirement]
- Speaking Intermediate [Oxford Supp. Skills] pp.28-30
- The Intermediate Choice p.110
- Workout Intermediate pp.80-1

OLD AGE contd.

Upper Intermediate
- Look Ahead Upper Intermediate pp.84-85
- New First Certificate Masterclass pp.28-29
- The New Cambridge English Course 4 p.100

Advanced
- Focus On Advanced English pp.71-73
- Headway Advanced pp.48-49
- Language Issues pp.130-132
- Proficiency Masterclass p.89

PARANORMAL

Pre-Intermediate
- Language In Use Pre-Intermediate pp.40-41

Early/Mid-Intermediate
- Look Ahead Intermediate pp.52-53

Upper Intermediate
- Look Ahead Upper Intermediate pp.106-107 [mediums]
- Think First Certificate [Revised] pp.148-157

Advanced
- Proficiency Masterclass pp.43-56
- Speaking Personally pp.49-51
- The Nelson Proficiency Course pp.181-197

PLACES

Beginner/Elementary
- Elementary Communication Games No.12
- Headway Elementary pp.73-75
- Look Ahead 1 pp.86-87 [Leeds Castle]
- The Beginners' Choice pp.116-118
- True To Life Elementary pp.81-85

Pre-Intermediate
- A Way With Words 1 pp.77-83
- Blueprint Two pp.11-12 [Oxford],27-28 [Scotland]
- Headway Pre-Intermediate pp.41-43,46 [Madrid v. London]
- Language In Use Pre-Intermediate pp.64-67
- Look Ahead 2 pp.68-69 [country v. city life]
- Reward Pre-Intermediate pp.22-23
- Test Your Vocabulary 1 pp.42-43
- Workout Pre-Intermediate p.104

Early/Mid-Intermediate
- Headway Intermediate p.28 [China]
- Intermediate Matters pp.55-60
- Meanings Into Words Intermediate pp.1-7
- New Headway Intermediate pp. [New York and London]
- The New Cambridge English Course 3 pp.80-81
- Think Ahead to First Certificate pp.68-75 [cities]

Upper Intermediate
- Blueprint Upper Intermediate pp.93-95
- First Certificate Gold pp.136-138
- New First Certificate Masterclass pp.16-20
- Workout Upper Intermediate pp.36-37

Advanced
- Distinction pp.141-147 [architecture]
- Headway Advanced pp.95-101
- The Nelson Proficiency Course pp.2-3 [city life]
- Workout Advanced pp.70-71,74-75

Various
- Discussions That Work p.55 [study spot the difference]

POLITICS

Beginner/Elementary
- Reading Elementary [Oxford Supp. Skills] pp.38-39 [Nelson Mandela]

Pre-Intermediate
- The Pre-Intermediate Choice p.78-82

Early/Mid-Intermediate
- Intermediate Vocabulary pp.12,17 [international relations]
- The Intermediate Choice p.72
- The New Cambridge English Course 3 pp.64-65
- Vocabulary Builder 2 pp.74-75

Upper Intermediate
- English Vocabulary In Use pp.108-109
- Headway Upper Intermediate pp.104-105 [interview with Margaret Thatcher]
- Look Ahead Upper Intermediate pp.10-13
- Meanings Into Words Upper Intermediate pp.50-51

POLITICS contd.

Advanced
- Advanced Vocabulary and Idiom pp.108-109
- English Vocabulary In Use pp.108-109
- Phrasal Verbs and Idioms [Making Headway] pp.20-24,52-57
- Speaking Personally p.4
- The Listening File pp.8-11 [interview with Diane Abbott]
- The Nelson Proficiency Course pp.129-130

Various
- The Q Book pp.74-75
- Writing Games Activity No.8

PREDICTING THE FUTURE

Beginner/Elementary
- True To Life Elementary pp.148-152

Pre-Intermediate
- Headway Pre-Intermediate pp.65-66
- Reward Pre-Intermediate pp.78-79

Early/Mid-Intermediate
- Headway Intermediate p.71
- Intermediate Matters pp.69-70,74
- Look Ahead Intermediate pp.88-93
- Think Ahead to First Certificate pp.114-115
- Workout Intermediate p.36

Upper Intermediate
- Blueprint Upper Intermediate pp.79-83
- Headway Upper Intermediate pp.56-59
- Look Ahead Upper Intermediate pp.112-119
- The New Cambridge English Course 4 p.101
- Think First Certificate [Revised] pp.174-185

Advanced
- Speaking Personally pp.8-12

PREJUDICE

Early/Mid-Intermediate
- Intermediate Matters pp.131-137
- Think Ahead to First Certificate pp.76-85

RELIGION

Advanced
- Headway Advanced (Adv.) pp.125-130

RESTAURANTS

Beginner/Elementary
- Elementary Task Listening pp.24-25
- Blueprint One pp.99-100
- The New Cambridge English Course 1 p.84
- Streamline Departures Unit 11

Pre-Intermediate
- Pre-Intermediate Matters p.36
- Streamline Connections Units 49,70
- The Pre-Intermediate Choice pp.32-33
- True To Life Pre-Intermediate pp.60-61

Early/Mid-Intermediate
- Everyday Listening and Speaking - Making Headway pp.19-22
- Intermediate Vocabulary p.14
- Workout Intermediate p.90

Upper Intermediate
- Blueprint Upper Intermediate pp.51-53
- Look Ahead Upper Intermediate pp.28-29,39

Advanced
- Progress To Proficiency (New Edition) pp.66-67
- Workout Advanced p.84

ROYALTY

Beginner/Elementary
- Reading Elementary [Oxford Supp. Skills] pp.18-19

Early/Mid-Intermediate
- Think Ahead to First Certificate pp.118-127

Upper Intermediate
- The New Cambridge English Course 4 pp.36-37 [man who broke into Buckingham Palace]

SCIENCE AND TECHNOLOGY

Beginner/Elementary
- Listening Elementary [Oxford Supp. Skills] pp.44-49
- Speaking Elementary [Oxford Supp. Skills] pp.16-17 [robots]

Pre-Intermediate
- Workout Pre-Intermediate p.62 [genetic engineering]

Early/Mid-Intermediate
- Headway Intermediate pp.73-76 [computers]
- Intermediate Vocabulary p.37 [computers]
- Look Ahead Intermediate pp.116-117 [computers]
- Workout Intermediate pp.12-13 [electronic equipment]

Upper Intermediate
- A Way With Words 3 pp.71-75
- English Vocabulary In Use pp.104-105
- First Certificate Gold p.38
- Listening Upper Intermediate [Oxford Supp. Skills] pp.22-24,46-50
- Meanings Into Words Upper Intermediate pp.29-30 [computers],80/81 [dishwashers]
- New First Certificate Masterclass pp.119-121 [computer games]
- Upper Intermediate Matters pp.120-121 ['cryonics']

Advanced
- English Vocabulary In Use pp.104-105
- Focus On Proficiency pp.100-101 [computer hacking],154-172
- Proficiency Masterclass pp.14-17 [Stephen Hawking]
- Progress To Proficiency (New Edition) pp.176-190

SELLING

Early/Mid-Intermediate
- Look Ahead Intermediate pp.42-44
- The Intermediate Choice p.16
- True To Life Intermediate pp.74-78,116-117

Upper Intermediate
- First Certificate Gold pp.120-123

Advanced
- Advanced Communication Games No.27
- Distinction pp.132-140
- Focus On Proficiency pp.173-194
- Phrasal Verbs and Idioms [Making Headway] pp.46-51
- Proficiency Masterclass pp.143-157
- The Nelson Proficiency Course pp.160-167
- Workout Advanced p.39

SHOPS/SHOPPING

Beginner/Elementary
- Blueprint One pp.51-52,115-116
- Elementary Communication Games Nos.9,10
- Elementary Task Listening pp.16-17,28-29
- Elementary Vocabulary pp.6-7
- Look Ahead 1 pp.54-59
- Start Testing Your Vocabulary p.39
- The Beginners' Choice pp.13,16,112
- The New Cambridge English Course 1 pp.33,49-50
- True To Life Elementary pp.124-125

Pre-Intermediate
- A Way With Words 1 pp.12-17
- Headway Pre-Intermediate pp.29-30 [Marks and Spencer]
- Language In Use Pre-Intermediate p.59 [the shopping game]
- Pre-Intermediate Matters p.12
- Streamline Connections Unit 78
- Test Your Vocabulary 1 pp.17,27-28
- The New Cambridge English Course 2 pp.34-35
- The Pre-Intermediate Choice pp.62,75,117
- True To Life Pre-Intermediate pp.50-52

Early/Mid-Intermediate
- Everyday Listening and Speaking - Making Headway pp.23-26
- Intermediate Matters pp.84-88
- Intermediate Vocabulary p.23
- Look Ahead Intermediate pp.40-41
- New Blueprint Intermediate pp.18-19
- Task Listening pp.32-33
- True To Life Intermediate pp.74-78,114-115
- Vocabulary Builder 2 pp.62-63
- Workout Intermediate p.97

Upper Intermediate
- First Certificate Gold pp.94-95

SHOPS/SHOPPING contd.

Advanced
- Progress To Proficiency (New Edition) pp.94-110

Various
- Discussions That Work pp.95-96
- Grammar Practice Activities pp.90-93
- The Q Book pp.27-29

SLEEP

Pre-Intermediate
- Streamline Connections Unit 8

Early/Mid-Intermediate
- Intermediate Matters pp.90-91 [in bed for 56 years]
- Vocabulary Builder 2 pp.12-13

Upper Intermediate
- New First Certificate Masterclass pp.158-159

Various
- The Q Book pp.117-120

SMOKING

Beginner/Elementary
- Reading Elementary [Oxford Supp. Skills] pp.26-27

Early/Mid-Intermediate
- Intermediate Vocabulary p.15
- Help With Phrasal Verbs pp.54-58
- New Headway Intermediate pp.100-102

Upper Intermediate
- New First Certificate Masterclass pp.105-107,110-111
- Think First Certificate [Revised] p.91
- Workout Upper Intermediate p.102

Advanced
- Focus On Proficiency pp.74-75
- The Listening File pp.52-55

Various
- The Q Book p.130

SPACE

Pre-Intermediate
- Streamline Connections Unit 12

Early/Mid-Intermediate
- Vocabulary Builder 2 pp.76-77
- Headway Intermediate pp.66-68
- Language In Use Intermediate pp.108-109 [asteroids]
- Meanings Into Words Intermediate pp.155-156 [Venus]

Upper Intermediate
- Meanings Into Words Upper Intermediate pp.140-142
- New First Certificate Masterclass pp.138-139
- Upper Intermediate Matters pp.54-55

Advanced
- Advanced Vocabulary and Idiom p.24
- Wordbuilder p.77

SPORT

Beginner/Elementary
- Elementary Vocabulary pp.16-17
- Look Ahead 1 p.70
- Play Games With English 2 pp.54-55
- Speaking Elementary [Oxford Supp. Skills] pp.12-13
- The New Cambridge English Course 1 p.109
- True To Life Elementary pp.88-89

Pre-Intermediate
- A Way With Words 1 pp.71-76
- Blueprint Two pp.83-84 [Ayrton Senna]
- Everyday Listening and Speaking - Making Headway pp.43-45 [going to the gym]
- Language In Use Pre-Intermediate p.73
- Pre-Intermediate Matters pp.115 [football],118
- Test Your Vocabulary 1 p.12
- The Pre-Intermediate Choice p.37 [football]
- Workout Pre-Intermediate pp.82-85

Early/Mid-Intermediate
- Headway Intermediate pp.3,12-13 [children in sport]
- Help With Phrasal Verbs pp.9-12 [violence at football matches]
- Intermediate Vocabulary p.24
- Meanings Into Words Intermediate p.177 [cycling]
- New Blueprint Intermediate pp.48-49,53

SPORT contd.

The Index: *Topics*

STRANGE EXPERIENCES

SUPERSTITION

TELEVISION

THEATRE (SEE CINEMA)

TIME

Beginner/Elementary
- Blueprint One pp.35-36
- Elementary Communication Games No.5
- Headstart p.36
- Headway Elementary p.24
- Look Ahead 1 pp.62-63
- Play Games With English 1 pp.80-81
- Streamline Departures Unit 26
- The Beginners' Choice pp.12-15,63
- The New Cambridge English Course 1 p.29

Pre-Intermediate
- A Way With Words 1 pp.33-36
- Headway Pre-Intermediate p.92
- Reward Pre-Intermediate pp.76-77 [time travellers]
- The Pre-Intermediate Choice pp.26,49,81
- True To Life Pre-Intermediate pp.133-137

Upper Intermediate
- Headway Upper Intermediate pp.99-100
- Look Ahead Upper Intermediate p.119 [time travel]

Advanced
- Advanced Vocabulary and Idiom pp.26,69-70
- Focus On Advanced English pp.15-20
- Language Issues pp.122-123 [time capsule competition]
- Proficiency Masterclass pp.16,66-67 [time travel]
- Wordbuilder pp.191-195

Various
- More Grammar Games pp.100-102

TRANSPORT

Beginner/Elementary
- Elementary Task Listening pp.38-39 [hiring a bike]
- The Beginners' Choice p.75

Pre-Intermediate
- A Way With Words 1 pp.42-46
- Headway Pre-Intermediate pp.105-107 [flying]
- Language In Use Pre-Intermediate pp.20-23
- Look Ahead 2 pp.24-25

- Pre-Intermediate Matters pp.30-34
- The New Cambridge English Course 2 pp.32-33
- The Pre-Intermediate Choice p.20
- Workout Pre-Intermediate pp.48-51

Early/Mid-Intermediate
- Everyday Listening and Speaking - Making Headway pp.7-10
- Help With Phrasal Verbs pp.21-22,32-34
- Intermediate Vocabulary pp.21,46
- Language In Use Intermediate pp.56-57 [passenger lands plane]
- Speaking Intermediate [Oxford Supp. Skills] pp.6-13
- Task Listening pp.2-3 [catching the right train],4-5 [catching a plane]
- Test Your Vocabulary 2 p.52
- The Intermediate Choice p.114

Upper Intermediate
- First Certificate Gold pp.13-14
- Headway Upper Intermediate pp.39,43 [lorry driver]
- New First Certificate Masterclass pp.124-126
- Upper Intermediate Matters pp.49,52

Advanced
- Distinction pp.24-25 [fear of flying]
- Progress To Proficiency (New Edition) pp.85-90

TRAVEL

Beginner/Elementary
- Elementary Communication Games Nos.17,18 [asking for travel information],23 [travelling to work]
- Elementary Task Listening pp.2-3 [changing travellers cheques],6-7 [coming through immigration],10-11 [checking flight departure time]
- Look Ahead 1 pp.8-11 [at the airport]
- The New Cambridge English Course 1 p.51
- True To Life Elementary pp.112-116

Pre-Intermediate
- Everyday Listening and Speaking - Making Headway pp.9-14,31-33 [at the travel agent's]
- Look Ahead 2 pp.24-29
- Reward Pre-Intermediate pp.30-31,68-69 [flying]

TRAVEL contd.

- Streamline Connections Unit 25 [by air]
- The New Cambridge English Course 2 pp.106-107
- True To Life Pre-Intermediate pp.83-87
- Workout Pre-Intermediate pp.20,73

Early/Mid-Intermediate
- A Way With Words 2 pp.18-22
- Headway Intermediate pp.22-23
- Intermediate Vocabulary pp.5 (air travel),27
- Listening Intermediate [Oxford Supp. Skills] pp.4-9
- Look Ahead Intermediate pp.26/27 [air travel],120-125
- New Headway Intermediate p.55
- Task Listening pp.30-31 [making enquiries at a travel agency]
- Vocabulary Builder 1 pp.68-69

Upper Intermediate
- A Way With Words 3 pp.38-41
- Headway Upper Intermediate pp.40-41 [bad flying experiences], 43
- Look Ahead Upper Intermediate pp.24-25 [flight attendants],32-37
- New First Certificate Masterclass pp.63-67
- The New Cambridge English Course 4 pp.108-109
- Think First Certificate [Revised] pp.68-71
- Upper Intermediate Matters pp.61-67

Advanced
- Advanced Communication Games No.29
- Distinction pp.24-29,60-67
- English Vocabulary In Use pp.98-99
- Focus On Advanced English pp.47-54 [air travel]
- Focus On Proficiency pp.38-54
- Proficiency Masterclass pp.59-69
- Progress To Proficiency (New Edition) pp.79-93
- Test Your Vocabulary 4 p.2
- Wordbuilder pp.178-180
- Workout Advanced pp.24,25,28,29,30

Various
- Discussions That Work pp.54 [railway station spot the difference],93-95
- The Q Book pp.136-138 [rail travel]

UFOs

Pre-Intermediate
- Headway Pre-Intermediate p.91
- Streamline Connections Unit 52

Early/Mid-Intermediate
- Intermediate Communication Games No.8

Upper Intermediate
- Meanings Into Words Upper Intermediate p.67
- Upper Intermediate Matters p.59

Advanced
- Speaking Personally pp.52-53
- The Nelson Proficiency Course pp.185-187

VIRTUAL REALITY

Upper Intermediate
- First Certificate Gold pp.36-37

WAR

Early/Mid-Intermediate
- Intermediate Vocabulary p.28

Advanced
- Headway Advanced pp.52-58
- Proficiency Masterclass pp.28-30
- Progress To Proficiency (New Edition) pp.260-264
- The Nelson Proficiency Course pp.36,149 [air raids in Manchester]

WEATHER

Beginner/Elementary
- Blueprint One pp.57-58
- Elementary Vocabulary p.5
- Headway Elementary p.88
- Look Ahead 1 pp.80-81
- Start Testing Your Vocabulary pp.18-19
- The Beginners' Choice pp.78-81
- True To Life Elementary pp.136-140

WEATHER contd.

Pre-Intermediate
- Blueprint Two p.68
- Look Ahead 2 pp.109,112-113
- Reward Pre-Intermediate pp.86-87
- Streamline Connections Unit 48
- True To Life Pre-Intermediate pp.70-74

Early/Mid-Intermediate
- Headway Intermediate p.25
- Intermediate Matters pp.33-34
- New Headway Intermediate p.50
- Task Listening pp.6-7
- The Intermediate Choice pp.50-51
- The New Cambridge English Course 3 pp.94-95
- Vocabulary Builder 1 pp.62-63

Upper Intermediate
- First Certificate Gold pp.110-113
- New First Certificate Masterclass pp.21-22,25

Advanced
- Distinction pp.96-103
- English Vocabulary In Use pp.64-65
- Focus On Advanced English pp.7-14
- Proficiency Masterclass pp.30,37-40

WOMEN/SEXISM

Beginner/Elementary
- Reading Elementary [Oxford Supp. Skills] pp.16-17 [female bus driver]

Pre-Intermediate
- Headway Pre-Intermediate pp.74-75 [suffragette movement]

Early/Mid-Intermediate
- Look Ahead Intermediate pp.34-35 [women police officers]
- New Blueprint Intermediate pp.36-37 [female motorcycle courier]
- Think Ahead to First Certificate p.85

Upper Intermediate
- A Way With Words 3 pp.91-94
- Blueprint Upper Intermediate pp.32-33 [female detectives]
- New First Certificate Masterclass pp.91-93
- Upper Intermediate Matters pp.32-35

Advanced
- Advanced Vocabulary and Idiom p.6
- Focus On Proficiency pp.23-24
- Language Issues pp.114-115
- Progress To Proficiency (New Edition) pp.40-43
- Reading Advanced [Oxford Supp. Skills] pp.1-16
- The Listening File pp.20-23
- The Nelson Proficiency Course pp.90-92

WORK/JOBS

Beginner/Elementary
- Blueprint One pp.23-24
- Elementary Vocabulary pp.8-9
- Listening Elementary [Oxford Supp. Skills] pp.8-13
- Look Ahead 1 pp.16-19,74-79
- Play Games With English 1 pp.10-11
- Play Games With English 2 p.15
- Speaking Elementary [Oxford Supp. Skills] pp.48-49
- Start Testing Your Vocabulary pp.12-13,16-17
- Streamline Departures Unit 4b
- The Beginners' Choice pp.34-35,76
- The New Cambridge English Course 1 p.10

Pre-Intermediate
- A Way With Words 1 pp.47-51
- Language In Use Pre-Intermediate pp.80-83
- Look Ahead 2 pp.48-49 [stuntman],54-55 [getting to work],100-101 [woman firefighter]
- Pre-Intermediate Matters p.52
- Test Your Vocabulary 1 pp.9-10,46-47
- The Pre-Intermediate Choice p.25
- Workout Pre-Intermediate pp.28,54

Early/Mid-Intermediate
- A Way With Words 2 pp.64-66
- Everyday Listening and Speaking - Making Headway pp.49-52
- Intermediate Vocabulary pp.30,38,49
- Language In Use Intermediate pp.40-41 [hated jobs]
- Look Ahead Intermediate pp.23,64-69
- Meanings Into Words Intermediate pp.16-20,95
- New Headway Intermediate pp.70-72 [servants]
- Speaking Intermediate [Oxford Supp. Skills] pp.33-39

WORK/JOBS contd.

- Test Your Vocabulary 2 p.11
- The Intermediate Choice p.24
- The New Cambridge English Course 3 pp.12-13 [pay]
- Think Ahead to First Certificate pp.53,80-81 [looking for a nanny]
- True To Life Intermediate pp.54-58,143-145 [job interviews]
- Vocabulary Builder 2 pp.56-59
- Workout Intermediate pp.48-50

Upper Intermediate
- A Way With Words 3 pp.29-33
- Blueprint Upper Intermediate pp.32-34
- First Certificate Gold pp.16-23
- Headway Upper Intermediate pp.20-26
- Listening Upper Intermediate [Oxford Supp. Skills] pp.8-12
- Look Ahead Upper Intermediate pp.40-45
- Meanings Into Words Upper Intermediate pp.6-7
- New First Certificate Masterclass pp.91-93
- Phrasal Verbs and Idioms [Making Headway] pp.53-58
- Test Your Vocabulary 3 pp.18-19
- The New Cambridge English Course 4 pp.38-39,58-59 [job interview]
- Think First Certificate [Revised] pp.80-81
- Upper Intermediate Matters pp.32-33,39-41 [job interviews]
- Workout Upper Intermediate pp.14-16

Advanced
- Advanced Communication Games No.38
- Advanced Vocabulary and Idiom p.74
- English Vocabulary In Use pp.80-81
- Focus On Proficiency pp.19-37,81-82 [nurses]
- Progress To Proficiency (New Edition) pp.203-218
- Test Your Vocabulary 4 p.59
- The Nelson Proficiency Course pp.20,25,27-29
- Wordbuilder pp.140-145

Various
- Grammar Practice Activities pp.257-258
- Keep Talking Activity Nos.53,57,64
- The Q Book pp.62-63

WORLD PROBLEMS

Upper Intermediate
- New First Certificate Masterclass pp.77-79
- Workout Upper Intermediate pp.84-86

Advanced
- English Vocabulary In Use pp.76-77
- Progress To Proficiency (New Edition) p.73 [food shortages]
- Workout Advanced p.62 [homelessness]

The Index: *Topics*

Section 4: Writing

DESCRIPTIVE contd.

Early/Mid-Intermediate
- Headway Intermediate p.13
- Look Ahead Intermediate pp.124-124 [places]
- Meanings Into Words Intermediate pp.116-117 [countries]
- New Headway Intermediate pp.22-23 [people],63/64 [rooms]
- Think Ahead to First Certificate pp.42 [favourite object],95 [places], 132 [rooms]

Upper Intermediate
- First Certificate Gold pp.81 [people],138 [places]
- New First Certificate Masterclass pp.18 [places],62 [objects], 103 [people],144
- Workout Upper Intermediate pp.54 [biographical description],82 [people]

Advanced
- Focus On Proficiency pp.6 [houses],68 [close friend]
- Proficiency Masterclass pp.24-25 [people],68-69,126-128
- The Nelson Proficiency Course p.96 [people]
- Workout Advanced p.36 [places]

DIALOGUE

Upper Intermediate
- Workout Upper Intermediate p.68

Advanced
- Workout Advanced p.115

DISCURSIVE

Early/Mid-Intermediate
- Headway Intermediate p.85
- New Headway Intermediate pp.114-115
- Think Ahead to First Certificate p.109
- Workout Intermediate p.76

Upper Intermediate
- Blueprint Upper Intermediate p.115
- First Certificate Gold pp.63,126-8, 156
- Headway Upper Intermediate pp.62-63
- New First Certificate Masterclass pp.115-117
- Think First Certificate [Revised] pp.88-89,112-113,122-123,147,182-183
- Upper Intermediate Matters p.126
- Writing Upper Intermediate [Oxford Supp. Skills] pp.42-52

Advanced
- Distinction p.136
- Focus On Proficiency p.64
- Proficiency Masterclass pp.10-11,194-195

DRAFTING/REDRAFTING

Beginner/Elementary
- The Beginners' Choice p.123

Upper Intermediate
- First Certificate Gold p.31

FAXES

Early/Mid-Intermediate
- New Headway Intermediate pp.54-55

FORMAL LETTERS

Beginner/Elementary
- Look Ahead 1 p.65
- Writing Elementary [Oxford Supp. Skills] pp.25-31

Pre-Intermediate
- Pre-Intermediate Matters p.50
- Look Ahead 2 p.23 [requestion information]
- Streamline Connections Unit 59 [reserving a room in a hotel]
- Workout Pre-Intermediate p.54

Early/Mid-Intermediate
- Headway Intermediate pp.29,64
- Intermediate Matters pp.44-45
- New Headway Intermediate p.74
- Workout Intermediate pp.52,64
- Writing Intermediate [Oxford Supp. Skills] pp.35-44

Upper Intermediate
- Headway Upper Intermediate pp.26,53-54
- Upper Intermediate Matters p.82 [letter of opinion]
- Workout Upper Intermediate pp.26,60,96
- Writing Upper Intermediate [Oxford Supp. Skills] pp.32-41

MAKING YOUR WRITING MORE INTERESTING

NARRATIVES

NOTES/MESSAGES

PARAGRAPHS

POEMS

POSTCARDS

Beginner/Elementary
- Blueprint One p.44
- Headstart pp.27-28
- Look Ahead 1 p.85
- The New Cambridge English Course 1 p.73

Pre-Intermediate
- Look Ahead 2 p.57

Early/Mid-Intermediate
- Look Ahead Intermediate pp.28-29
- Writing Intermediate [Oxford Supp. Skills] pp.1-7

Various
- Writing Games Activity Nos.28,39

REPORTS

Early/Mid-Intermediate
- Intermediate Matters p.109

Upper Intermediate
- First Certificate Gold pp.72-73
- New First Certificate Masterclass pp.82-83,166,169-170
- Writing Upper Intermediate [Oxford Supp. Skills] pp.70-75

Advanced
- Focus On Proficiency pp.120-121,190
- Language Issues p.35
- Proficiency Masterclass pp.156-157
- Writing Advanced [Oxford Supp. Skills] pp.92-102

PUNCTUATION

Beginner/Elementary
- Elementary Vocabulary p.55
- Look Ahead 1 p.35 [capital letters]

Pre-Intermediate
- Headway Pre-Intermediate p.86 [apostrophes]
- Pre-Intermediate Matters p.8
- The Pre-Intermediate Choice p.103

Early/Mid-Intermediate
- Headway Intermediate p.36
- Intermediate Matters p.15
- Intermediate Vocabulary p.53
- Meanings Into Words Intermediate p.49
- Think Ahead to First Certificate pp.23,67

Upper Intermediate
- New First Certificate Masterclass p.20
- Writing Upper Intermediate [Oxford Supp. Skills] pp.77-80

Advanced
- Distinction p.37
- Headway Advanced pp.93-94
- Progress To Proficiency (New Edition) pp.43-44

REVIEWS

Pre-Intermediate
- Streamline Connections Unit 67

Upper Intermediate
- Blueprint Upper Intermediate pp.38-39 [film]
- Headway Upper Intermediate pp.35-36 [book or film]
- Upper Intermediate Matters p.23

Advanced
- Distinction pp.84-85 [film],129 [song]
- Focus On Advanced English pp.40-41 [book]
- Workout Advanced pp.84 [restaurants],99 [novels]

SELF-CORRECTION

Upper Intermediate
- Headway Upper Intermediate p.7
- New First Certificate Masterclass pp.188-189

SEQUENCERS

Pre-Intermediate
- The Pre-Intermediate Choice p.75

Early/Mid-Intermediate
- Meanings Into Words Intermediate pp.30-31
- Think Ahead to First Certificate p.19

SEQUENCERS contd.

Upper Intermediate
- First Certificate Gold p.24
- Meanings Into Words Upper Intermediate pp.105-113

Advanced
- Advanced Communication Games No.7

SPEECH

Upper Intermediate
- Workout Upper Intermediate p.88

SPELLING

Beginner/Elementary
- Elementary Vocabulary pp.56-61
- Essential Grammar In Use pp.220-221
- Play Games With English 1 pp.26-27,84-85
- Play Games With English 2 pp.46-47
- The Beginners' Choice p.4

Pre-Intermediate
- Headway Pre-Intermediate p.39

Early/Mid-Intermediate
- English Grammar In Use pp.280-281
- Intermediate Matters p.31

Upper Intermediate
- Headway Upper Intermediate p.34

Advanced
- Language Issues pp.57,86

SUMMARIES

Early/Mid-Intermediate
- Think Ahead to First Certificate pp.71,99

Upper Intermediate
- Upper Intermediate Matters p.87

Advanced
- Distinction pp.20,51
- Focus On Proficiency p.127
- Proficiency Masterclass pp.6-7,35-36, 50-51,64-66,77-79,108-109
- The Nelson Proficiency Course pp.14-15

TRANSACTIONAL LETTER

Upper Intermediate
- First Certificate Gold (U.Int.) pp.20-21,118
- New First Certificate Masterclass (U.Int.) pp.54-55,127

Section 5: Miscellaneous

- Learning English outside the classroom
- Useful language learning activities
- Improving reading skills
- Improving listening skills
- Improving writing skills
- Improving speaking skills
- Keeping a learner diary
- Learning vocabulary
- Learning grammar
- Using translation
- Making mistakes
- General

ABBREVIATIONS

Beginner/Elementary
- Elementary Vocabulary pp.53-54

Early/Mid-Intermediate
- Intermediate Vocabulary p.82

Advanced
- Advanced Vocabulary and Idiom pp.104-105
- English Vocabulary In Use pp.196-197

BRITISH V. AMERICAN ENGLISH

Pre-Intermediate
- Test Your Vocabulary 1 pp.55-56

Early/Mid-Intermediate
- English Grammar In Use pp.282-283
- Intermediate Vocabulary p.80
- Play Games With English 3 pp.68-69
- Test Your Vocabulary 2 p.45
- Vocabulary Builder 2 p.80

Upper Intermediate
- Test Your Vocabulary 3 p.62

Advanced
- English Vocabulary In Use pp.186-187
- Language Issues pp.78,83
- Proficiency Masterclass pp.133,136
- Test Your Vocabulary 4 p.42

DEDUCING WORDS FROM CONTEXT

Pre-Intermediate
- The Pre-Intermediate Choice p.31

Early/Mid-Intermediate
- Intermediate Matters p.105

Upper Intermediate
- Headway Upper Intermediate pp.12-13

Advanced
- Workout Advanced p.24

FALSE FRIENDS

Advanced
- Advanced Vocabulary and Idiom pp.48-52

FORMAL/INFORMAL LANGUAGE

Early/Mid-Intermediate
- Intermediate Vocabulary pp.77-79
- New Headway Intermediate p.115
- The New Cambridge English Course 3 p.102

Upper Intermediate
- First Certificate Gold p.118
- New First Certificate Masterclass pp.32-33

Advanced
- Advanced Vocabulary and Idiom pp.86-90
- English Vocabulary In Use pp.14-15
- Focus On Proficiency pp.12,33,49-50,68-69,88-89,106-108,128-129,145-149
- Headway Advanced pp.113-115
- Proficiency Masterclass pp.82-83

LEARNER TRAINING

Learning English outside the classroom

Pre-Intermediate
- The Pre-Intermediate Choice pp.122/3

Useful language learning activities

Early/Mid-Intermediate
- Workout Intermediate p.17

Improving reading skills

Beginner/Elementary
- The Beginners' Choice pp.90-91

Pre-Intermediate
- Blueprint Two p.80

Early/Mid-Intermediate
- Workout Intermediate p.29

Advanced
- Focus On Advanced English p.6
- Language Issues p.9

LEARNER TRAINING contd.

Improving listening skills

Beginner/Elementary
- The Beginners' Choice pp.90-91

Pre-Intermediate
- Blueprint Two p.64

Early/Mid-Intermediate
- Workout Intermediate p.41

Upper Intermediate
- Blueprint Upper Intermediate p.6

Advanced
- Focus On Advanced English p.26

Improving writing skills

Beginner/Elementary
- The Beginners' Choice p.123

Pre-Intermediate
- Blueprint Two p.96

Early/Mid-Intermediate
- The Intermediate Choice p.123
- Workout Intermediate p.53

Upper Intermediate
- Blueprint Upper Intermediate p.7

Advanced
- Focus On Advanced English pp.44-46
- Language Issues p.11

Improving speaking skills

Beginner/Elementary
- The Beginners' Choice p.122

Pre-Intermediate
- Blueprint Two pp.47-48
- True To Life Pre-Intermediate pp.10-11

Early/Mid-Intermediate
- Upper Intermediate Matters p.5
- The Intermediate Choice p.91

Upper Intermediate
- Blueprint Upper Intermediate p.6

Advanced
- Workout Advanced p.58

Keeping a learner diary

Early/Mid-Intermediate
- Intermediate Matters pp.30-31
- Workout Intermediate p.65

Learning vocabulary

Beginner/Elementary
- Blueprint One p.48
- The Beginners' Choice p.32

Pre-Intermediate
- A Way With Words 1 pp.2-4
- Headway Pre-Intermediate pp.17,37
- True To Life Pre-Intermediate pp.116-117

Early/Mid-Intermediate
- A Way With Words 2 pp.1-5
- The Intermediate Choice p.33
- Workout Intermediate p.77

Upper Intermediate
- A Way With Words 3 pp.1-3
- Blueprint Upper Intermediate p.7

Advanced
- English Vocabulary In Use pp.2-7
- Progress To Proficiency (New Edition) p.7

Learning grammar

Beginner/Elementary
- Blueprint One p.80
- The Beginners' Choice p.60

Early/Mid-Intermediate
- Intermediate Matters p.29
- The Intermediate Choice p.63
- Workout Intermediate p.89

Upper Intermediate
- Blueprint Upper Intermediate p.6

Using translation

Early/Mid-Intermediate
- Workout Intermediate p.96

Making mistakes

Advanced
- Workout Advanced p.100

LEARNER TRAINING contd.

General

Beginner/Elementary
- True To Life Elementary p.92

Pre-Intermediate
- Pre-Intermediate Matters p.125
- Blueprint Two p.16

Early/Mid-Intermediate
- Intermediate Matters p.30
- True To Life Intermediate pp.11-12

Advanced
- Focus On Advanced English pp.39-40

RECORDING NEW VOCABULARY

Beginner/Elementary
- The Beginners' Choice p.32
- Headway Elementary p.11

Pre-Intermediate
- Headway Pre-Intermediate p.17

Early/Mid-Intermediate
- Intermediate Matters p.23

Upper Intermediate
- First Certificate Gold p.7
- Headway Upper Intermediate p.6

USEFUL CLASSROOM LANGUAGE

Beginner/Elementary
- The Beginners' Choice p.5

USING A DICTIONARY

Beginner/Elementary
- The Beginners' Choice p.91
- Headway Elementary pp.10-11

Pre-Intermediate
- Blueprint Two p.32
- Headway Pre-Intermediate pp.10-11

Early/Mid-Intermediate
- A Way With Words 2 pp.4-5
- Intermediate Matters p.20

Upper Intermediate
- A Way With Words 3 p.4
- Upper Intermediate Matters p.8

Advanced
- English Vocabulary In Use pp.10-11
- Headway Advanced pp.8-9

WORD FORMATION

Beginner/Elementary
- Elementary Vocabulary pp.38-46
- Play Games With English 2 pp.72-73 [prefixes]

Early/Mid-Intermediate
- A Way With Words 2 pp.7-9,68-72
- Intermediate Matters pp.56,80
- Intermediate Vocabulary pp.55-76
- New Headway Intermediate p.42

Upper Intermediate
- A Way With Words 3 pp.42-44,114-119
- First Certificate Gold p.14
- New First Certificate Masterclass p.76
- Upper Intermediate Matters pp.13,122,129

Advanced
- Advanced Vocabulary and Idiom pp.29-40
- English Vocabulary In Use pp.16-39
- Headway Advanced p.45
- Language Issues p.86
- Progress To Proficiency (New Edition) p.57 [forming adjectives],182-183 [suffixes]

Various
- Grammar Games pp.42-44

WORDS OFTEN CONFUSED

Early/Mid-Intermediate
- Test Your Vocabulary 2 pp.48-49
- Intermediate Vocabulary pp.84-88

Upper Intermediate
- Test Your Vocabulary 3 pp.71-72

WORDS OFTEN CONFUSED contd.

Advanced
- Advanced Vocabulary and Idiom pp.41-45
- Progress To Proficiency (New Edition) pp.28-29
- Test Your Vocabulary 4 pp.23-24
- Test Your Vocabulary 5 pp.36-37

Reader's Notes

Reader's Notes